Ukulele Chord Dictionary

All the essential chords in
an easy-to-follow format!

Alfred Music Co., Inc.
P.O. Box 10003
Van Nuys, CA 91410-0003
alfred.com

ISBN-10: 0-7390-9527-7
ISBN-13: 978-0-7390-9527-0

Cover photo courtesy of the Martin Guitar Company.

 Alfred Cares. Contents printed on environmentally responsible paper.

Contents

Introduction

Alfred's Mini Music Guide *Ukulele Chord Dictionary* provides the most essential chords and chordal information in a portable, handy size, and it is loaded with a variety of fingerings for the most important chords in all 12 keys.

Starting on page 22, the chords are listed alphabetically and chromatically for quick reference (A♭, A, B♭, B, etc.). On each page, the chord fingerings are arranged in a logical order, starting from the lowest position on the fingerboard to the highest. Within each key, the chords progress from the most basic major and minor chords all the way up to 7ths, 9ths, and even altered chords.

For each chord, there is an illustrated chord diagram with fingerings and note names; see pages 20–21 for an explanation of how to read these.

The first part of this book (pages 6–21) makes it easy to understand intervals and how chords are constructed. Theory on triads, seventh chords, extended chords, altered chords, and other chord types are covered.

You can refer to the section on moveable chords (starting on page 214), which will maximize your knowledge by showing how to play 12 different chords with a single fingering. Once you understand basic chord theory and the concept of moveable chords, you can take the chords in this book and use them to fit any performance situation. *Ukulele Chord Dictionary* provides the basis for an ever-growing chord vocabulary that can be applied in all musical styles.

IMPORTANT NOTE: There are four basic types of four-string ukuleles, from smallest to largest: *soprano*, *concert* (sometimes called *alto*), *tenor*, and *baritone*. The soprano, concert, and tenor sizes can be tuned identically, and any of these three are appropriate for the chords in this book (though it may be difficult to reach some of the higher chords with a soprano ukulele, which usually has only 12 frets). The baritone uke is tuned differently (like the first four strings of a guitar) and cannot be used to play the chords in this dictionary.

In addition, there are several ukulele tuning variants. *Ukulele Chord Dictionary* uses the most common standard tuning for the soprano, concert, and tenor ukulele: the G–C–E–A tuning, with a high G. This is also sometimes called C or C6 tuning, because the open notes form a C6 chord.

Chord Theory

Intervals

Play any note on the ukulele, then play a note one fret above it. The distance between these two notes is a *half step*. Play another note followed by a note two frets above it. The distance between these two notes is a *whole step* (two half steps). The distance between any two notes is referred to as an *interval*.

In the example of the C major scale below, the letter names are shown above the notes and the *scale degrees* (numbers) of the notes are written below. Notice that C is the first degree of the scale, D is the second, etc.

The name of an interval is determined by counting the number of scale degrees from one note to the next. For example, an interval of a 3rd, starting on C, would be determined by counting up three scale degrees, or C–D–E (1–2–3). C to E is a 3rd. An interval of a 4th, starting on C, would be determined by counting up four scale degrees, or C–D–E–F (1–2–3–4). C to F is a 4th.

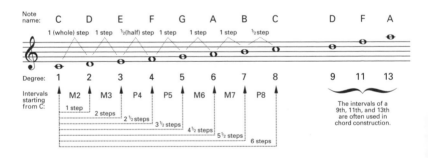

As shown above, intervals are not only labeled by the distance between scale degrees, but by the *quality* of the interval. An interval's quality is determined by counting the number of whole steps and half steps between the two notes of an interval. For example, C to E is a 3rd. C to E is also a major third because there are two whole steps between C and E. Likewise, C to E♭ is a 3rd, but C to E♭ is also a minor third because there are 1½ steps between C and E♭. There are five qualities used to describe intervals: *major, minor, perfect, diminished,* and *augmented.*

M	=	Major	o =	Diminished (dim)
m	=	Minor	+ =	Augmented (aug)
P	=	Perfect		

Particular intervals are associated with certain qualities:

2nds, 9ths	=	Major, Minor, and Augmented
3rds, 6ths, 13ths	=	Major, Minor, Augmented, and Diminished
4ths, 5ths, 11ths	=	Perfect, Augmented, and Diminished
7ths	=	Major, Minor, and Diminished

When a major interval is made *smaller* by a half step it becomes a *minor* interval.

When a *minor* interval is made *larger* by a half step it becomes a *major* interval.

When a *minor* or *perfect* interval is made *smaller* by a half step it becomes a *diminished* interval.

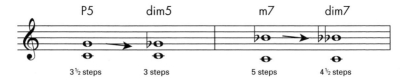

When a *major* or *perfect* interval is made *larger* by a half step it becomes an *augmented* interval.

Below is a table of intervals starting on the note C. Notice that some intervals are labeled *enharmonic*, which means they are written differently but sound the same (see aug2 and m3).

Table of Intervals

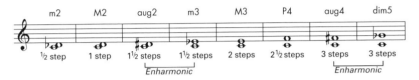

	m2	M2	aug2	m3	M3	P4	aug4	dim5
	½ step	1 step	1½ steps	1½ steps	2 steps	2½ steps	3 steps	3 steps
			Enharmonic				*Enharmonic*	

	P5	aug5	m6	M6	dim7	m7	M7	P8
	3½ steps	4 steps	4 steps	4½ steps	4½ steps	5 steps	5½ steps	6 steps
		Enharmonic			*Enharmonic*			

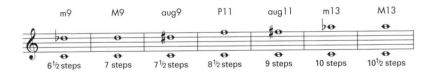

	m9	M9	aug9	P11	aug11	m13	M13
	6½ steps	7 steps	7½ steps	8½ steps	9 steps	10 steps	10½ steps

Basic Triads

A *chord* consists of two or more notes played together. Most commonly, a chord will have three or more notes. A three-note chord is called a *triad*. The *root* of a triad (or any other chord) is the note from which a chord is constructed. The relationship of the intervals from the root to the other notes of a chord determines the chord *type*. Triads are most frequently identified as one of four chord types: *major*, *minor*, *diminished*, and *augmented*.

All chord types can be identified by the intervals used to create the chord. For example, the C major triad is built beginning with C as the root, adding a major 3rd (E), and adding a perfect 5th (G). All major triads contain a root, M3, and P5.

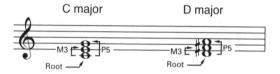

Minor triads contain a root, minor 3rd, and perfect 5th. (An easier way to build a minor triad is to simply lower the 3rd of a major triad.) All minor triads contain a root, m3, and P5.

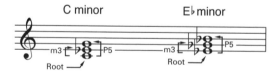

Diminished triads contain a root, minor 3rd, and diminished 5th. If the perfect 5th of a minor triad is made smaller by a half step (to become a diminished 5th), the result is a diminished triad. All diminished triads contain a root, m3, and dim5.

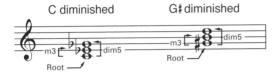

Augmented triads contain a root, major 3rd, and augmented 5th. If the perfect 5th of a major triad is made larger by a half step (to become an augmented 5th), the result is an augmented triad. All augmented triads contain a root, M3, and aug5.

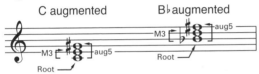

An important concept to remember about chords is that the bottom note of a chord will *not* always be the root. If the root of a triad, for instance, is moved above the 5th so that the 3rd is the bottom note of the chord, it is said to be in the *first inversion*. If the root and 3rd are moved above the 5th, the chord is in the *second inversion*. The number of inversions that a chord can have is related to the number of notes in the chord: a three-note chord can have two inversions, a four-note chord can have three inversions, etc.

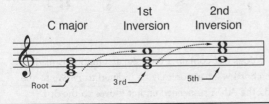

Building Chords

By using the four chord types as basic building blocks, it is possible to create a variety of chords by adding 6ths, 7ths, 9ths, and even 11ths and 13ths. Following are examples of some of the many variations.

* The *suspended fourth* chord does not contain a third. An assumption is made that the 4th degree of the chord will harmonically be inclined to *resolve* to the 3rd degree. In other words, the 4th is *suspended* until it moves to the 3rd.

Up until now, the examples have shown intervals and chord construction based on C. Until you are familiar with all the chords, the C chord examples on the previous pages can serve as a reference guide when building chords based on other notes: For instance, locate C7(♭9). To construct a G7(♭9) chord, first determine what intervals are contained in C7(♭9), then follow the steps outlined on the next page.

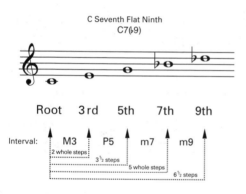

Now, let's figure out how to construct a G7(♭9) chord:

1. Determine the *root* of the chord. A chord is always named for its root—in this case, G is the root of G7(♭9).

2. Count *letter names* up from the *letter name of the root* (G), as we did when building intervals on page 6, to determine the intervals of the chord. Counting three letter names up from G to B (G–A–B, 1–2–3) is a 3rd, G to D (G–A–B–C–D) is a 5th, G to F is a 7th, and G to A is a 9th.

3. Determine the *quality* of the intervals by counting whole steps and half steps up from the root; G to B (2 whole steps) is a major 3rd, G to D (3½ steps) is a perfect 5th, G to F (5 whole steps) is a minor 7th, and G to A♭ (6½ steps) is a minor 9th.

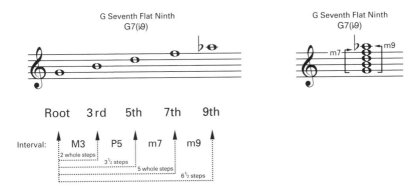

Follow this general guideline to figure out the notes of any chord. As interval and chord construction become more familiar, it will become possible to create your own original fingerings on the ukulele. Feel free to experiment!

The Circle of 5ths

Ukulele Chord Dictionary is organized to provide the fingerings of chords in all keys. The *circle of 5ths* below will help to clarify which chords are enharmonic equivalents (notice that *chords* can be written enharmonically as well as *notes*, see page 9). The circle of 5ths also serves as a quick reference guide to the relationship of the keys and how *key signatures* can be figured out. (A key signature, which indicates the key, is a group of sharps or flats at the beginning of a staff. Note: The key signature for C has no sharps or flats.) Clockwise movement (up a P5) provides all of the sharp keys by adding one sharp to the key signature. Counterclockwise (down a P5) provides the flat keys by adding one flat.

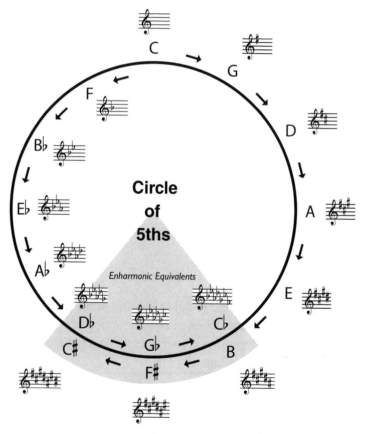

Reading Chords
Chord Symbol Variations

Chord symbols are a form of musical shorthand that give ukulele players as much information about a chord as quickly as possible. Since chord symbols are not universally standardized, they are often written in many different ways—some are understandable, others are confusing. To illustrate this point, below is a listing of some of the ways copyists, composers, and arrangers have created variations on the more common chord symbols.

C	Csus	C(♭5)	C(add9)
C major Cmaj CM	Csus4 C(addF) C4	C-5 C(5-) C(♯4)	C(9) C(add2) C(+9) C(+D)
C5	**Cm**	**C+**	**C°**
C(no3) C(omit3)	Cmin Cmi C-	C+5 Caug Caug5 C(♯5)	C° C°7 C7°
C6	**C6/9**	**Cm6/9**	**Cm6**
Cmaj6 C(addA) C(A)	C6(add9) C6(addD) C9(no7) C9/6	C-6/9 Cm6(+9) Cm6(add9) Cm6(+D)	C-6 Cm(addA) Cm(+6)

C7	C7sus	Cm7	Cm7($\flat$5)
C(addB$\flat$)	C7sus4	Cmi7	Cmi7-5
C7̶	Csus7	Cmin7	C-7(5-)
C(-7)	C7(+4)	C-7	C∅
C(+7)		C7mi	C ½dim

C7+	C7($\flat$5)	Cmaj7	Cmaj7($\flat$5)
C7+5	C7-5	Cma7	Cmaj7(-5)
C7aug	C7(5-)	C7̶	C7̶(-5)
C7aug5	C7̶-5	C△	C△($\flat$5)
C7($\sharp$5)	C7($\sharp$4)	C△7	

Cm(maj7)	C7($\flat$9)	C7($\sharp$9)	C7+($\flat$9)
C-maj7	C7(-9)	C7(+9)	Caug7-9
C-7̶	C9$\flat$	C9$\sharp$	C+7($\flat$9)
Cmi7̶	C9-	C9+	C+9$\flat$
			C7+(-9)

Cm9	C9	C9+	C9($\flat$5)
Cm7(9)	C_7^9	C9(+5)	C9(-5)
Cm7(+9)	C7add9	Caug9	$C7_{-5}^9$
C-9	C7(addD)	C($\sharp$9$\sharp$5)	C9(5$\flat$)
Cmi7(9+)	C7(+9)	C+9	

Cmaj9	C9($\sharp$11)	Cm9(maj7)	C11
C$\overline{7}$(9)	C9(+11)	C-9($\sharp$7)	C9(11)
C$\overline{7}$(+9)	C($\sharp$11)	C(-9)$\overline{7}$	C9addF
C9(maj7)	C11+	Cmi9($\sharp$7)	C9+11
C$\overline{9}$	C11$\sharp$		$C7_{11}^9$

Cm11	C13	C13($\flat$9)	C13($_{\flat 5}^{\flat 9}$)
C-11	C9addA	C13(-9)	C13(-9-5)
Cm($\flat$11)	C9(6)	$C_{\flat 9}^{13}$	C($\flat$9$\flat$5)addA
Cmi7$_9^{11}$	C7addA	C($\flat$9)addA	
C-7($_{11}^9$)	C7+A		

Chord Frames

Ukulele *chord frames* are diagrams that contain all the information necessary to play a particular chord. The fingerings, note names, and position of the chord on the neck are all provided on the chord frame (see next page). The photo below shows which number corresponds to which fretting-hand finger.

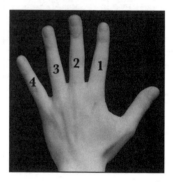

To provide smoother and more comfortable transitions between chords in a progression, choose chord positions that require the least motion from one chord to the next; select fingerings that are in approximately the same location on the neck of the ukulele.

The illustrations on the next page explain the various chord frame symbols.

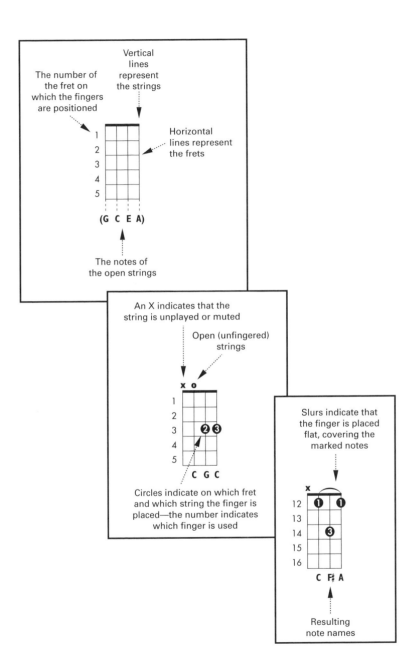

The number of the fret on which the fingers are positioned

Vertical lines represent the strings

Horizontal lines represent the frets

(G C E A)

The notes of the open strings

An X indicates that the string is unplayed or muted

Open (unfingered) strings

C G C

Circles indicate on which fret and which string the finger is placed—the number indicates which finger is used

Slurs indicate that the finger is placed flat, covering the marked notes

C F♯ A

Resulting note names

21

Chords in All 12 Keys

Ab

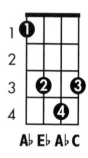

Ab Eb Ab C

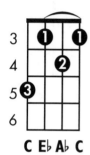

C Eb Ab C

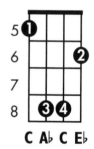

C Ab C Eb

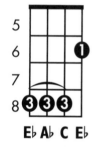

Eb Ab C Eb

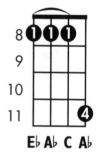

Eb Ab C Ab

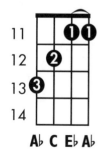

Ab C Eb Ab

A♭m

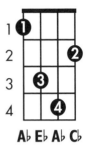

A♭ E♭ A♭ C♭

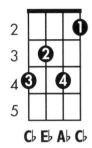

C♭ E♭ A♭ C♭

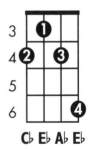

C♭ E♭ A♭ E♭

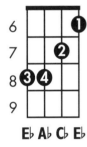

E♭ A♭ C♭ E♭

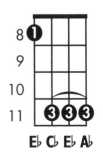

E♭ C♭ E♭ A♭

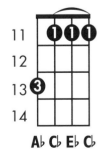

A♭ C♭ E♭ C♭

23

A♭°

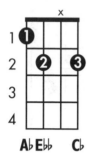

A♭ E♭♭   C♭

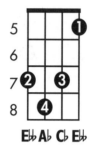

E♭♭ A♭ C♭ E♭♭

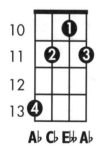

A♭ C♭ E♭♭ A♭

A♭+

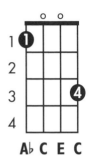

A♭ C E C

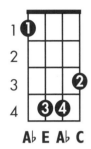

A♭ E A♭ C

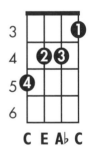

C E A♭ C

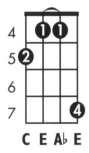

C E A♭ E

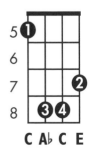

C A♭ C E

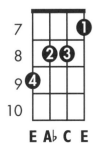

E A♭ C E

25

Ab5

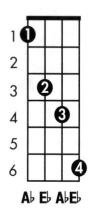

Ab Eb AbEb

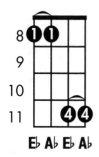

Eb Ab Eb Ab

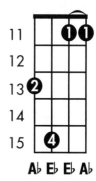

Ab Eb Eb Ab

A♭sus4

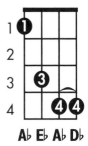

A♭ E♭ A♭ D♭

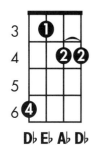

D♭ E♭ A♭ D♭

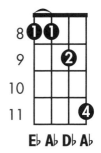

E♭ A♭ D♭ A♭

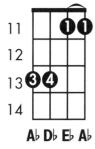

A♭ D♭ E♭ A♭

Ab6

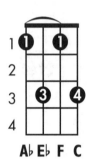

Ab Eb F C

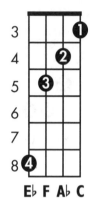

Eb F Ab C

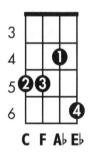

C F Ab Eb

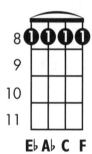

Eb Ab C F

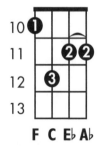

F C Eb Ab

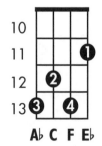

Ab C F Eb

A♭m6

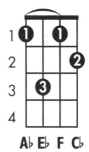

A♭ E♭ F C♭

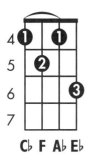

C♭ F A♭ E♭

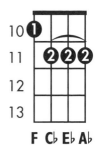

F C♭ E♭ A♭

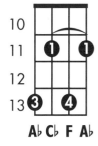

A♭ C♭ F A♭

A♭7

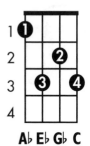

A♭ E♭ G♭ C

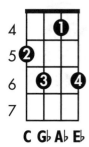

C G♭ A♭ E♭

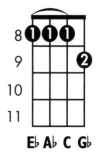

E♭ A♭ C G♭

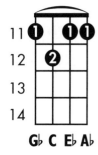

G♭ C E♭ A♭

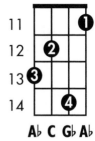

A♭ C G♭ A♭

A♭maj7

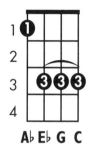

A♭ E♭ G C

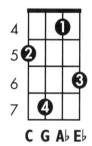

C G A♭ E♭

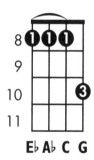

E♭ A♭ C G

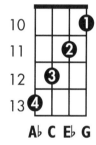

A♭ C E♭ G

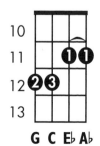

G C E♭ A♭

A♭m7

Ab

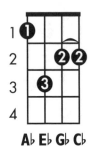

A♭ E♭ G♭ C♭

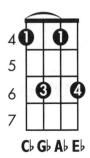

C♭ G♭ A♭ E♭

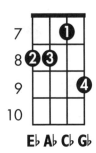

E♭ A♭ C♭ G♭

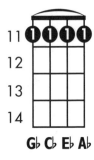

G♭ C♭ E♭ A♭

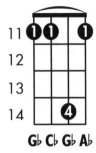

G♭ C♭ G♭ A♭

32

A♭m7(♭5)

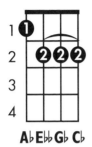

A♭ E♭♭ G♭ C♭

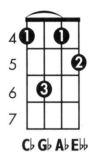

C♭ G♭ A♭ E♭♭

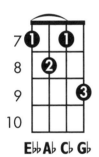

E♭♭ A♭ C♭ G♭

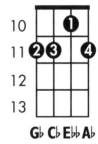

G♭ C♭ E♭♭ A♭

Ab°7

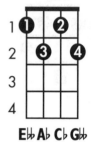

Eꞵꞵ Aꞵ Cꞵ Gꞵꞵ

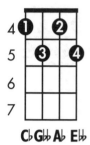

Cꞵ Gꞵꞵ Aꞵ Eꞵꞵ

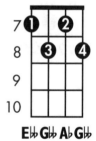

Eꞵꞵ Gꞵꞵ Aꞵ Gꞵꞵ

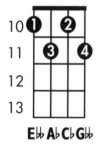

Eꞵꞵ Aꞵ Cꞵ Gꞵꞵ

A♭(add9)

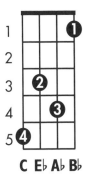

C E♭ A♭ B♭

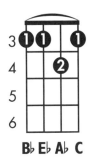

B♭ E♭ A♭ C

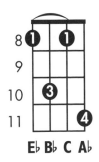

E♭ B♭ C A♭

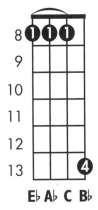

E♭ A♭ C B♭

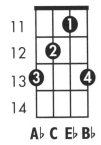

A♭ C E♭ B♭

Ab9

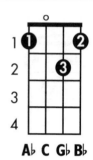

Ab C Gb Bb

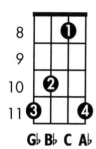

Gb Bb C Ab

Abmaj9

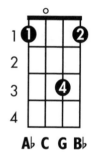

Ab C G Bb

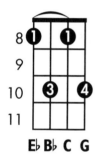

Eb Bb C G

Abm9

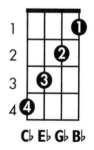

Cb Eb Gb Bb

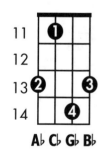

Ab Cb Gb Bb

A♭7+

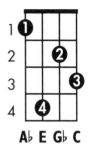

A♭ E G♭ C

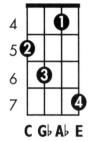

C G♭ A♭ E

A♭7(♭9)

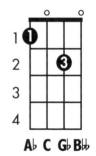

A♭ C G♭ B♭♭

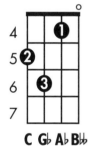

C G♭ A♭ B♭♭

A♭7(♯9)

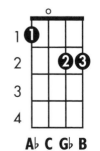

A♭ C G♭ B

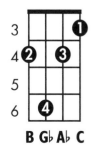

B G♭ A♭ C

A

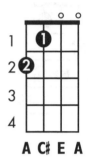

A C# E A

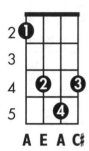

A E A C#

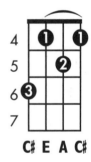

C# E A C#

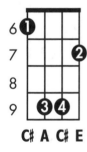

C# A C# E

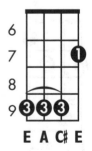

E A C# E

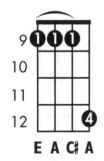

E A C# A

Am

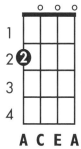

A C E A

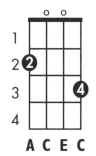

A C E C

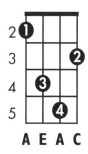

A E A C

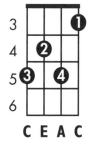

C E A C

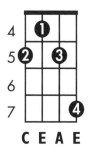

C E A E

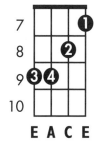

E A C E

A°

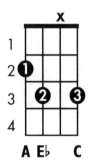

A E♭ C

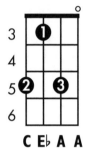

C E♭ A A

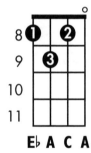

E♭ A C A

40

A+

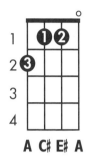

A C# E# A

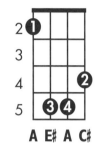

A E# A C#

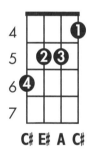

C# E# A C#

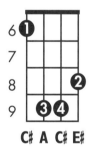

C# A C# E#

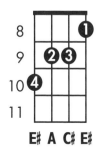

E# A C# E#

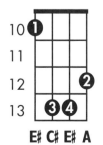

E# C# E# A

A5

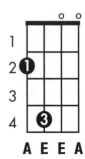

A E E A

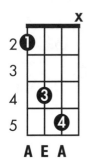

A E A

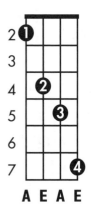

A E A E

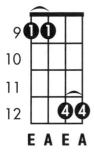

E A E A

Asus4

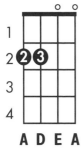

A D E A

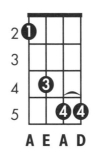

A E A D

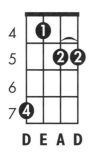

D E A D

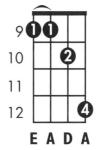

E A D A

A6

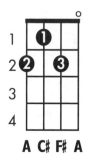

A C# F# A

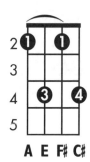

A E F# C#

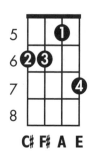

C# F# A E

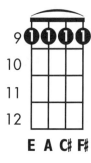

E A C# F#

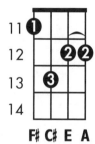

F# C# E A

Am6

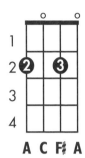

A C F# A

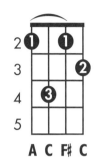

A C F# C

A

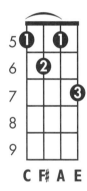

C F# A E

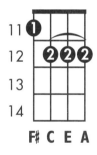

F# C E A

A7

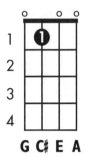

G C# E A

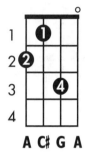

A C# G A

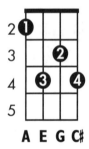

A E G C#

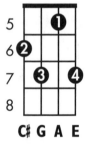

C# G A E

Amaj7

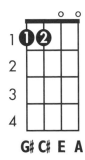

G# C# E A

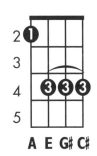

A E G# C#

A

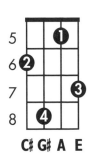

C# G# A E

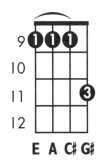

E A C# G#

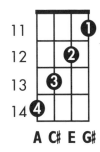

A C# E G#

Am7

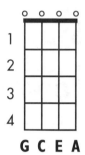

G C E A

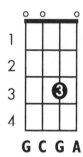

G C G A

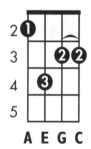

A E G C

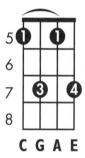

C G A E

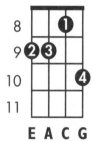

E A C G

48

Am7(♭5)

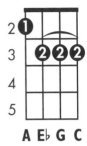

A E♭ G C

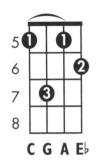

C G A E♭

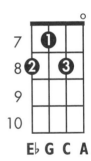

E♭ G C A

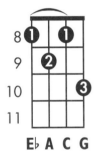

E♭ A C G

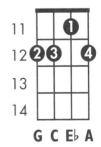

G C E♭ A

A°7

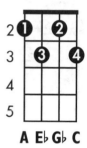

A Eb Gb C

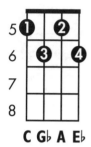

C Gb A Eb

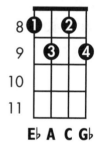

Eb A C Gb

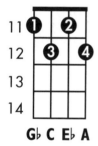

Gb C Eb A

A(add9)

A C# E B

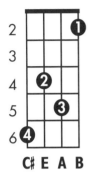

C# E A B

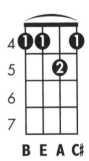

B E A C#

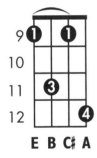

E B C# A

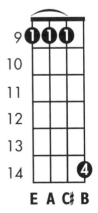

E A C# B

A

51

A9

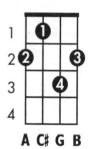

A C# G B

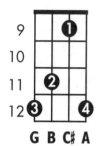

G B C# A

Amaj9

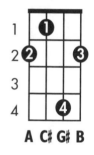

A C# G# B

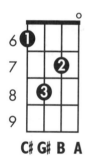

C# G# B A

Am9

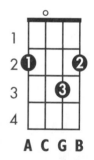

A C G B

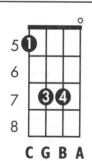

C G B A

A7+

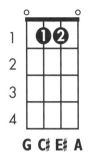

G C# E# A

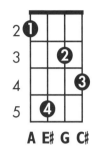

A E# G C#

A7(♭9)

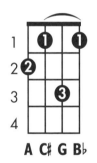

A C# G B♭

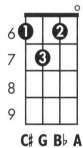

C# G B♭ A

A7(#9)

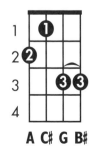

A C# G B#

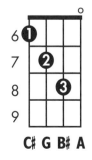

C# G B# A

B♭

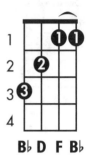

B♭ D F B♭

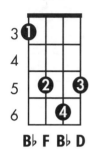

B♭ F B♭ D

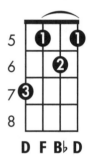

D F B♭ D

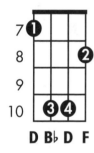

D B♭ D F

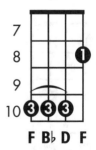

F B♭ D F

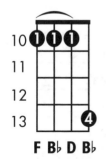

F B♭ D B♭

B♭m

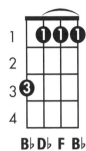

B♭ D♭ F B♭

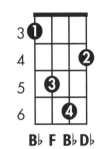

B♭ F B♭ D♭

B♭

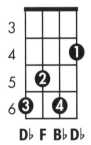

D♭ F B♭ D♭

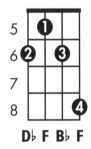

D♭ F B♭ F

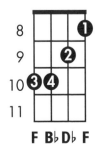

F B♭ D♭ F

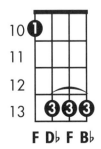

F D♭ F B♭

B♭°

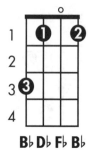

B♭ D♭ F♭ B♭

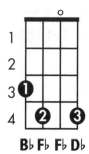

B♭ F♭ F♭ D♭

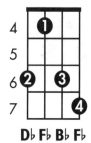

D♭ F♭ B♭ F♭

B♭+

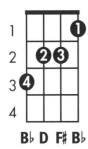

B♭ D F♯ B♭

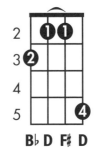

B♭ D F♯ D

B♭

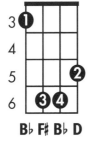

B♭ F♯ B♭ D

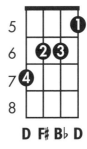

D F♯ B♭ D

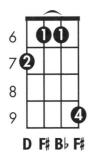

D F♯ B♭ F♯

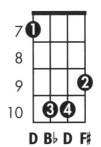

D B♭ D F♯

57

Bb5

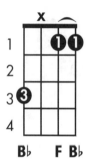

Bb   F Bb

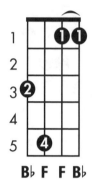

Bb F F Bb

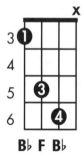

Bb F Bb

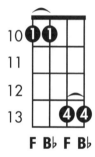

F Bb F Bb

B♭sus4

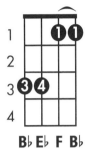

B♭ E♭ F B♭

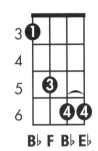

B♭ F B♭ E♭

B♭

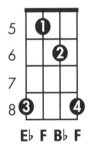

E♭ F B♭ F

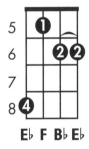

E♭ F B♭ E♭

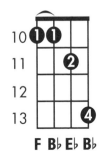

F B♭ E♭ B♭

B♭6

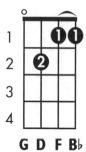

G D F B♭

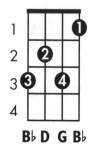

B♭ D G B♭

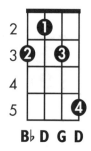

B♭ D G D

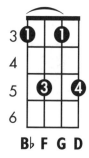

B♭ F G D

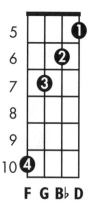

F G B♭ D

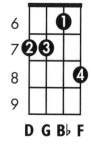

D G B♭ F

B♭m6

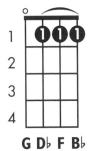

G D♭ F B♭

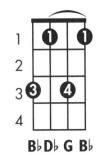

B♭ D♭ G B♭

B♭

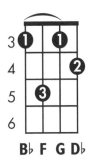

B♭ F G D♭

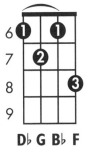

D♭ G B♭ F

B♭7

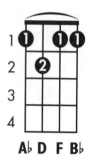

A♭ D F B♭

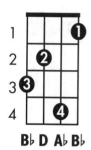

B♭ D A♭ B♭

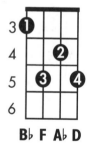

B♭ F A♭ D

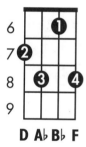

D A♭ B♭ F

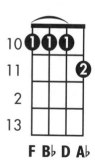

F B♭ D A♭

B♭maj7

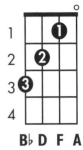

B♭ D F A

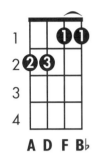

A D F B♭

B♭

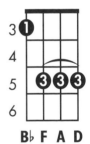

B♭ F A D

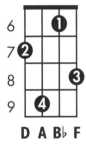

D A B♭ F

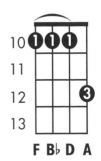

F B♭ D A

B♭m7

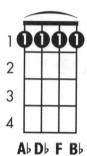

A♭ D♭ F B♭

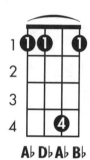

A♭ D♭ A♭ B♭

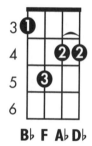

B♭ F A♭ D♭

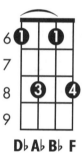

D♭ A♭ B♭ F

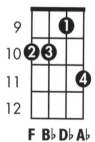

F B♭ D♭ A♭

B♭m7(♭5)

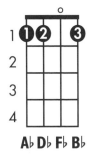

A♭ D♭ F♭ B♭

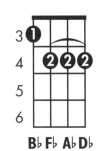

B♭ F♭ A♭ D♭

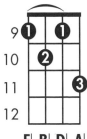

F♭ B♭ D♭ A♭

B♭

B♭°7

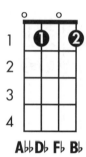

A♭♭ **D**♭ **F**♭ **B**♭

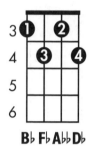

B♭ **F**♭ **A**♭♭ **D**♭

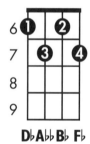

D♭ **A**♭♭ **B**♭ **F**♭

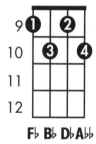

F♭ **B**♭ **D**♭ **A**♭♭

B♭(add9)

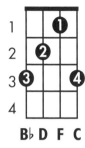

B♭ D F C

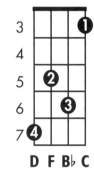

D F B♭ C

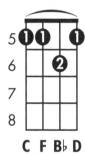

C F B♭ D

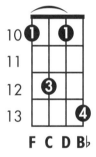

F C D B♭

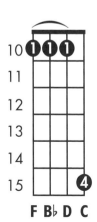

F B♭ D C

Bb9

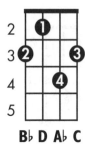

Bb D Ab C

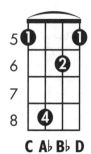

C Ab Bb D

Bbmaj9

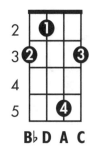

Bb D A C

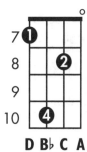

D Bb C A

Bbm9

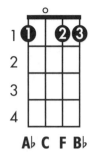

Ab C F Bb

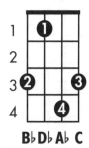

Bb Db Ab C

Bb7+

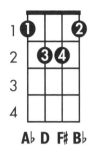

Ab D F# Bb

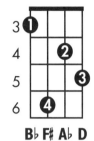

Bb F# Ab D

Bb

Bb7(b9)

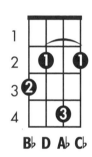

Bb D Ab Cb

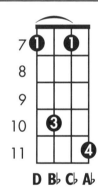

D Bb Cb Ab

Bb7(#9)

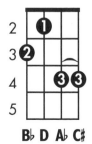

Bb D Ab C#

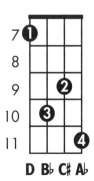

D Bb C# Ab

B

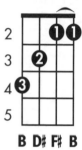

B D# F# B

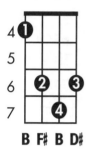

B F# B D#

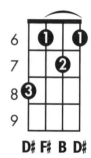

D# F# B D#

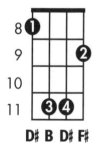

D# B D# F#

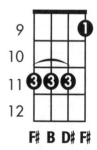

F# B D# F#

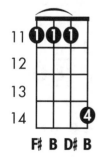

F# B D# B

Bm

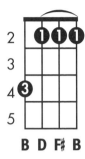

2
3
4
5

B D F# B

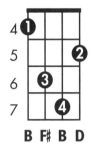

4
5
6
7

B F# B D

B

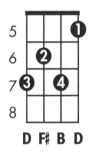

5
6
7
8

D F# B D

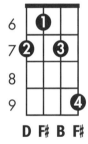

6
7
8
9

D F# B F#

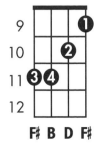

9
10
11
12

F# B D F#

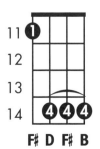

11
12
13
14

F# D F# B

B°

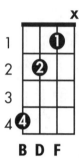

B D F

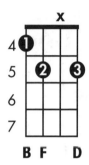

B F D

B

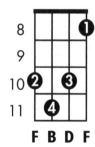

F B D F

B+

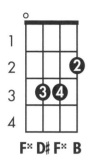

F× D♯ F× B

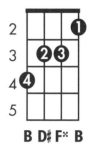

B D♯ F× B

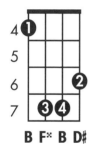

B F× B D♯

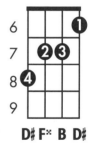

D♯ F× B D♯

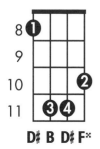

D♯ B D♯ F×

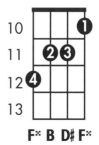

F× B D♯ F×

B5

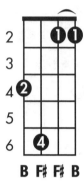

B F# F# B

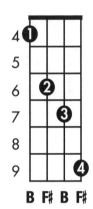

B F# B F#

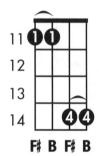

F# B F# B

Bsus4

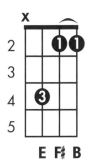

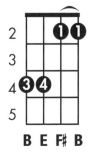

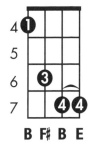

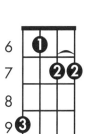

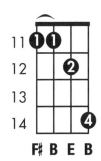

B6

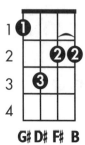

G# D# F# B

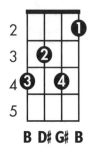

B D# G# B

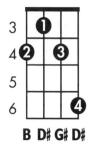

B D# G# D#

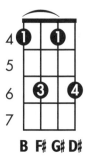

B F# G# D#

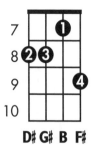

D# G# B F#

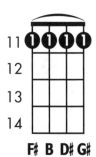

F# B D# G#

Bm6

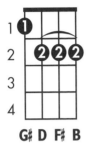

G# D F# B

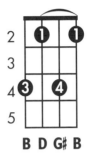

B D G# B

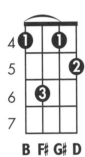

B F# G# D

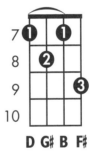

D G# B F#

B7

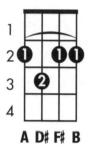

A D# F# B

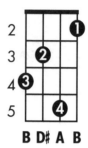

B D# A B

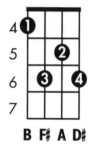

B F# A D#

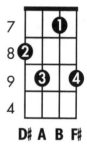

D# A B F#

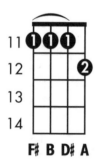

F# B D# A

Bmaj7

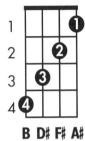

B D♯ F♯ A♯

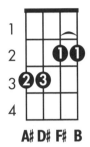

A♯ D♯ F♯ B

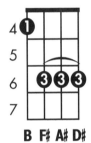

B F♯ A♯ D♯

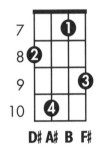

D♯ A♯ B F♯

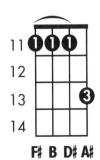

F♯ B D♯ A♯

Bm7

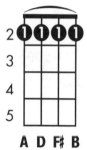

A D F# B

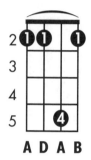

A D A B

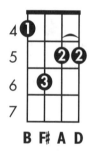

B F# A D

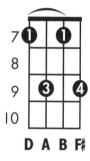

D A B F#

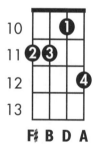

F# B D A

B

Bm7(♭5)

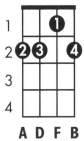

A D F B

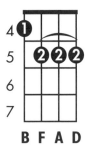

B F A D

B

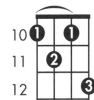

F B D A

B°7

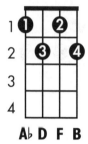

Ab D F B

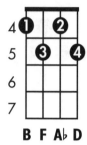

B F Ab D

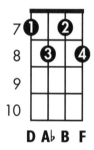

D Ab B F

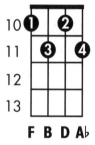

F B D Ab

B(add9)

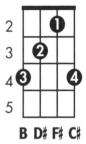

B D# F# C#

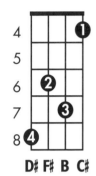

D# F# B C#

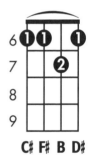

C# F# B D#

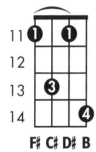

F# C# D# B

B

B9

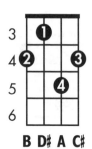

B D# A C#

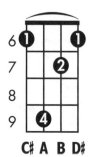

C# A B D#

Bmaj9

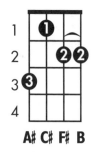

A# C# F# B

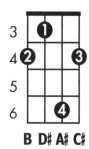

B D# A# C#

Bm9

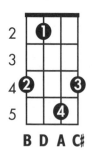

B D A C#

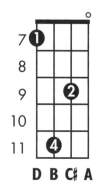

D B C# A

B

B7+

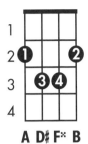

A D♯ F✻ B

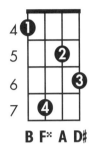

B F✻ A D♯

B7(♭9)

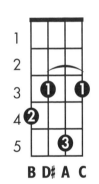

B D♯ A C

D♯ B C A

B7(♯9)

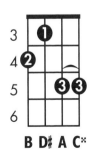

B D♯ A C✻

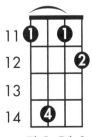

F♯ C✻ D♯ A

B

C

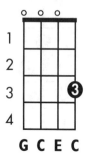

G C E C

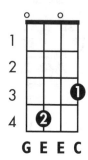

G E E C

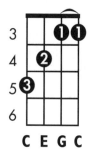

C E G C

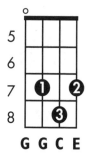

G G C E

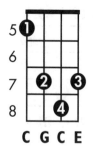

C G C E

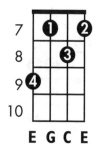

E G C E

Cm

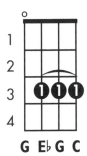

G E♭ G C

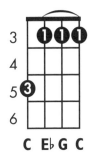

C E♭ G C

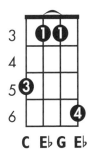

C E♭ G E♭

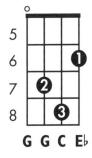

G G C E♭

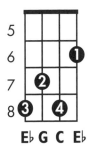

E♭ G C E♭

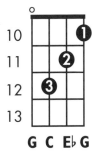

G C E♭ G

C

C°

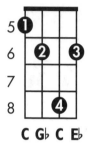

C Eb Gb C

C Gb C Eb

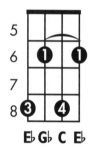

Eb Gb C Eb

C+

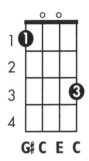

G# C E C

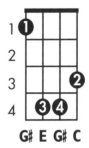

G# E G# C

C

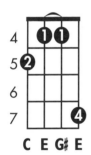

C E G# E

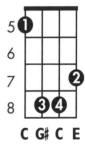

C G# C E

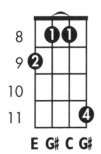

E G# C G#

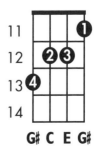

G# C E G#

C5

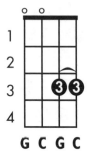

G C G C

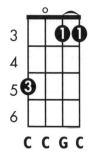

C C G C

C

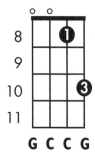

G C C G

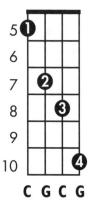

C G C G

Csus4

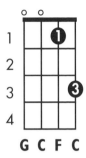

G C F C

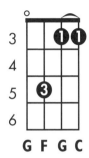

G F G C

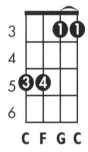

C F G C

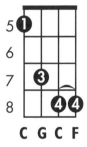

C G C F

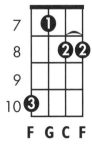

F G C F

C6

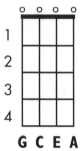

G C E A

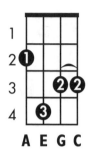

A E G C

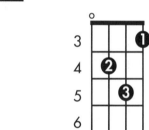

G E A C

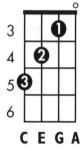

C E G A

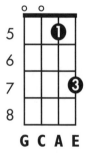

G C A E

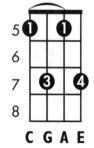

C G A E

C

Cm6

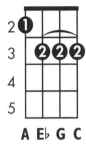

A E♭ G C

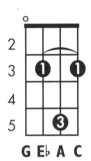

G E♭ A C

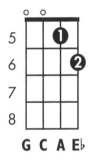

G C A E♭

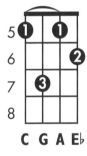

C G A E♭

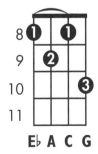

E♭ A C G

C

93

C7

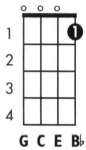

G C E B♭

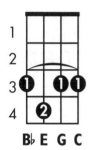

B♭ E G C

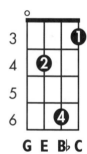

G E B♭ C

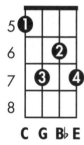

C G B♭ E

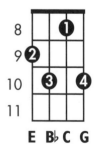

E B♭ C G

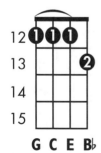

G C E B♭

C

Cmaj7

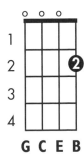

G C E B

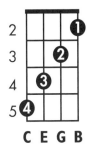

C E G B

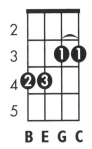

B E G C

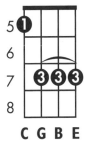

C G B E

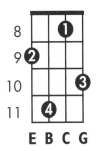

E B C G

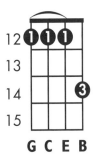

G C E B

C

Cm7

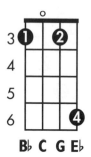

B♭ C G E♭

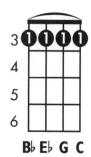

B♭ E♭ G C

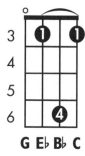

G E♭ B♭ C

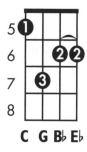

C G B♭ E♭

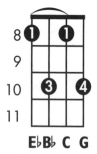

E♭ B♭ C G

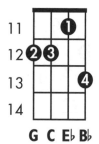

G C E♭ B♭

C

Cm7(♭5)

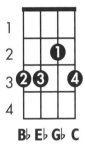

B♭ E♭ G♭ C

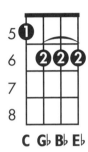

C G♭ B♭ E♭

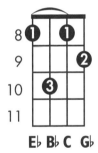

E♭ B♭ C G♭

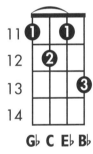

G♭ C E♭ B♭

C

C°7

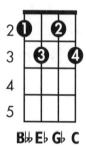

B♭♭ E♭ G♭ C

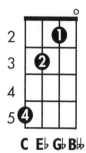

C E♭ G♭ B♭♭

C

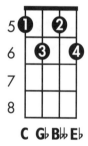

C G♭ B♭♭ E♭

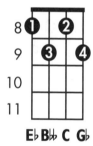

E♭ B♭♭ C G♭

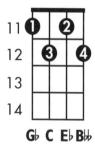

G♭ C E♭ B♭♭

C(add9)

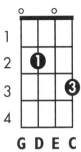

G D E C

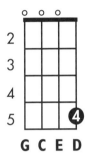

G C E D

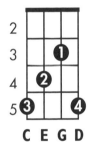

C E G D

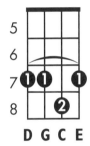

D G C E

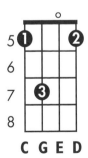

C G E D

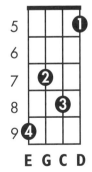

E G C D

C

C9

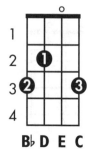

Bb D E C

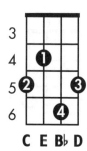

C E Bb D

Cmaj9

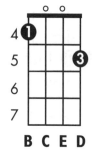

B C E D

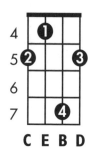

C E B D

Cm9

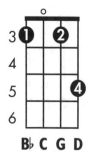

Bb C G D

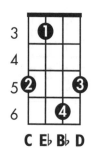

C Eb Bb D

C

C7+

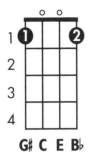

G# C E Bb

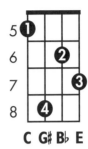

C G# Bb E

C7(b9)

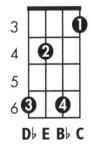

Db E Bb C

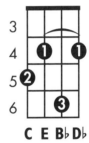

C E Bb Db

C7(#9)

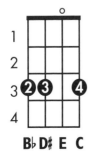

Bb D# E C

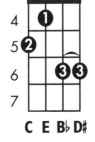

C E Bb D#

C

C#

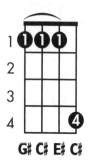

G# C# E# C#

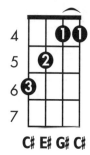

C# E# G# C#

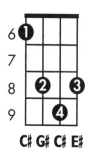

C# G# C# E#

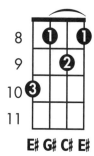

E# G# C# E#

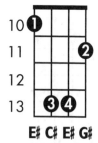

E# C# E# G#

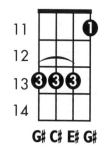

G# C# E# G#

C#m

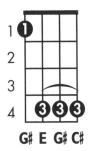

G# E G# C#

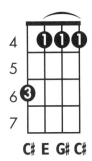

C# E G# C#

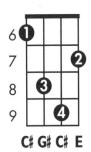

C# G# C# E

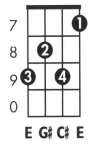

E G# C# E

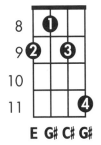

E G# C# G#

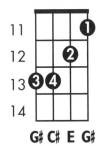

G# C# E G#

C#

C#°

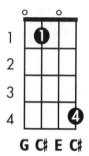

G C# E C#

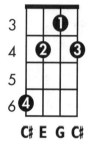

C# E G C#

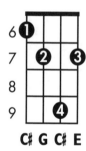

C# G C# E

C#+

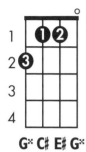

G× C# E# G×

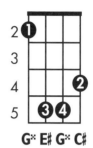

G× E# G× C#

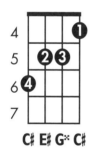

C# E# G× C#

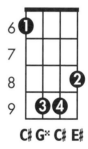

C# G× C# E#

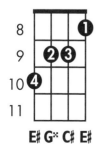

E# G× C# E#

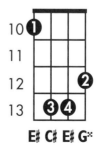

E# C# E# G×

C#

C#5

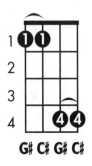

G# C# G# C#

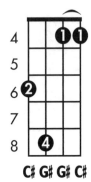

C# G# G# C#

C#

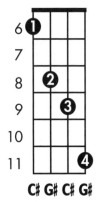

C# G# C# G#

C#sus4

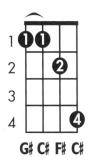

G# C# F# C#

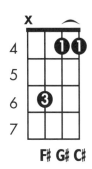

F# G# C#

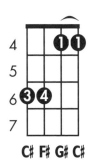

C# F# G# C#

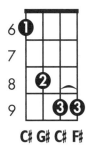

C# G# C# F#

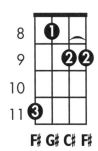

F# G# C# F#

C#6

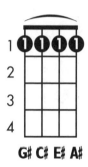

G# C# E# A#

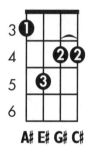

A# E# G# C#

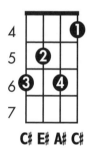

C# E# A# C#

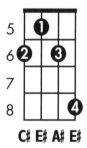

C# E# A# E#

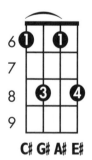

C# G# A# E#

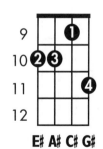

E# A# C# G#

C#m6

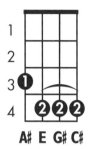

A# E G# C#

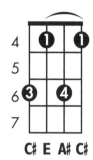

C# E A# C#

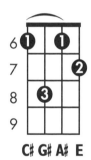

C# G# A# E

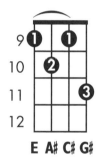

E A# C# G#

109

C#7

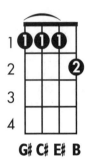

G# C# E# B

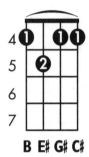

B E# G# C#

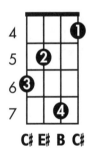

C# E# B C#

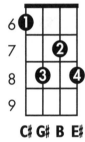

C# G# B E#

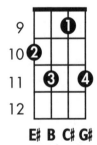

E# B C# G#

C#maj7

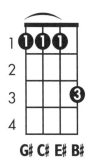

G# C# E# B#

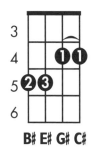

B# E# G# C#

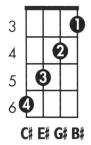

C# E# G# B#

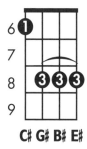

C# G# B# E#

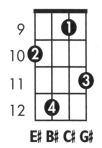

E# B# C# G#

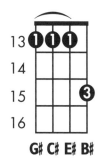

G# C# E# B#

C#

C#m7

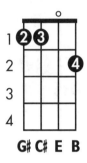

G# C# E B

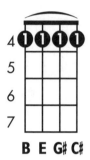

B E G# C#

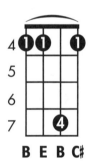

B E B C#

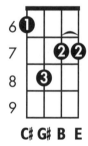

C# G# B E

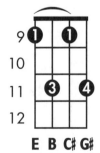

E B C# G#

C#m7(♭5)

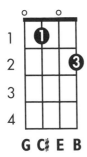

G C# E B

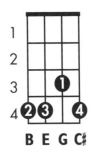

B E G C#

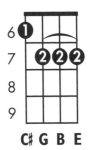

C# G B E

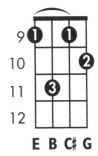

E B C# G

C#

C#°7

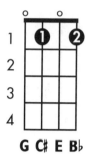

G C# E Bb

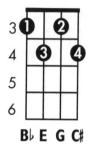

Bb E G C#

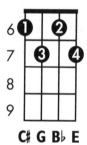

C# G Bb E

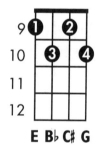

E Bb C# G

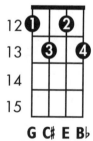

G C# E Bb

C#(add9)

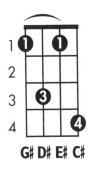

G# D# E# C#

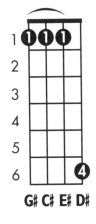

G# C# E# D#

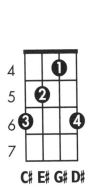

C# E# G# D#

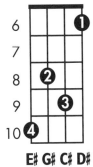

E# G# C# D#

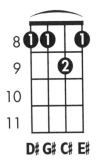

D# G# C# E#

C#

C#9

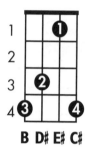

B D# E# C#

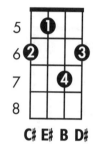

C# E# B D#

C#maj9

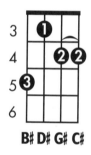

B# D# G# C#

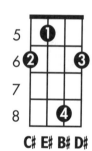

C# E# B# D#

C#m9

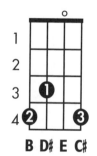

B D# E C#

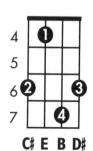

C# E B D#

C#

C#7+

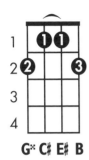

G✕ C# E# B

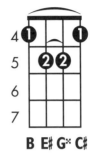

B E# G✕ C#

C#7(♭9)

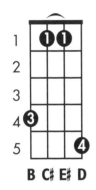

B C# E# D

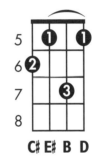

C# E# B D

C#7(#9)

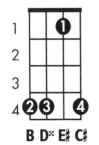

B D✕ E# C#

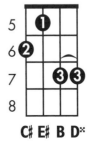

C# E# B D✕

C#

117

D

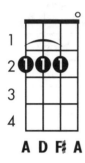

A D F# A

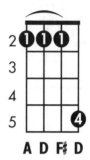

A D F# D

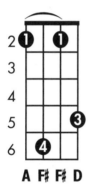

A F# F# D

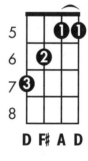

D F# A D

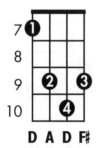

D A D F#

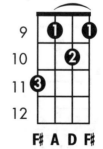

F# A D F#

Dm

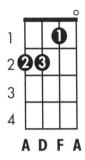

A D F A

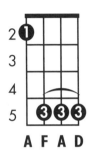

A F A D

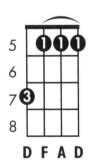

D F A D

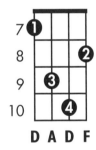

D A D F

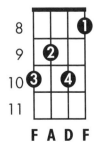

F A D F

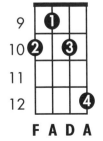

F A D A

D

D°

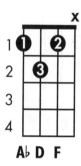

A♭ D F

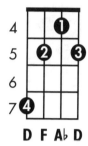

D F A♭ D

D

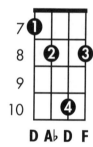

D A♭ D F

D+

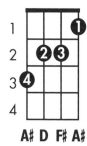

A# D F# A#

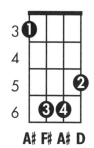

A# F# A# D

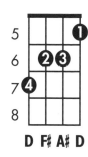

D F# A# D

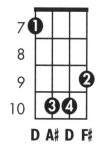

D A# D F#

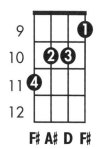

F# A# D F#

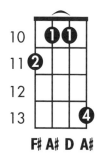

F# A# D A#

D

D5

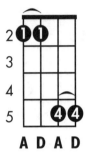

A D A D

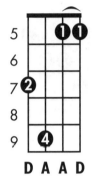

D A A D

D

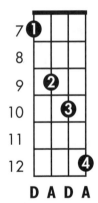

D A D A

Dsus4

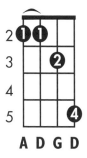

A D G D

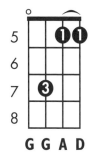

G G A D

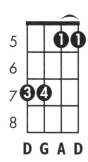

D G A D

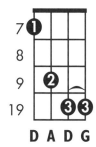

D A D G

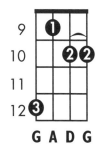

G A D G

D6

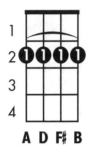

A D F# B

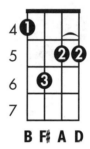

B F# A D

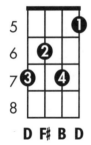

D F# B D

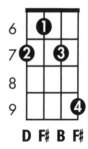

D F# B F#

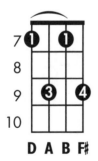

D A B F#

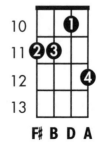

F# B D A

D

Dm6

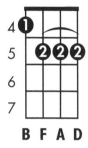

B F A D

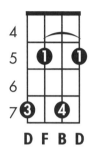

D F B D

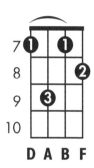

D A B F

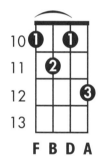

F B D A

D

D7

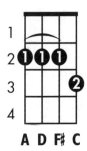

A D F# C

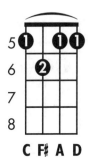

C F# A D

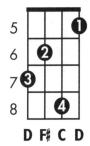

D F# C D

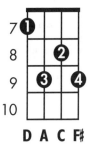

D A C F#

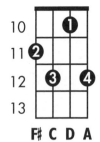

F# C D A

D

Dmaj7

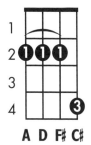

1
2 ❶❶❶
3
4 ❸

A D F♯ C♯

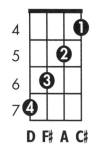

4 ❶
5 ❷
6 ❸
7 ❹

D F♯ A C♯

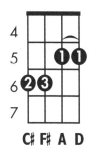

4
5 ❶❶
6 ❷❸
7

C♯ F♯ A D

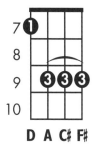

7 ❶
8
9 ❸❸❸
10

D A C♯ F♯

D

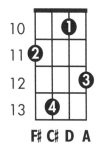

10 ❶
11 ❷
12 ❸
13 ❹

F♯ C♯ D A

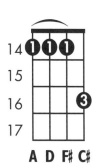

14 ❶❶❶
15
16 ❸
17

A D F♯ C♯

127

Dm7

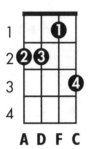

A D F C

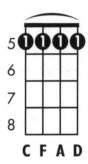

C F A D

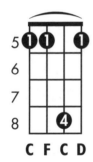

C F C D

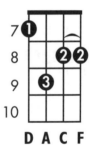

D A C F

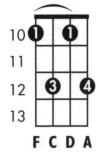

F C D A

D

Dm7(♭5)

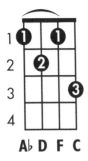

Ab D F C

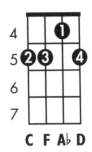

C F Ab D

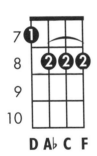

D Ab C F

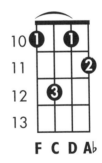

F C D Ab

D

D°7

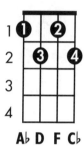

Ab D F Cb

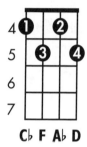

Cb F Ab D

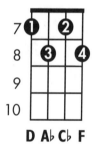

D Ab Cb F

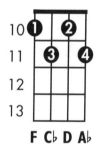

F Cb D Ab

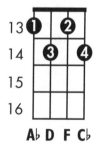

Ab D F Cb

D

D(add9)

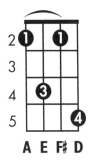

A E F# D

A D F# E

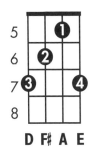

D F# A E

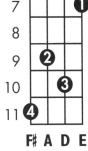

F# A D E

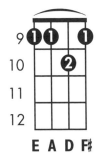

E A D F#

D

D9

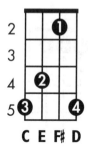

C E F# D

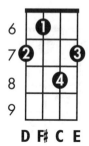

D F# C E

Dmaj9

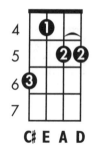

C# E A D

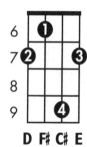

D F# C# E

Dm9

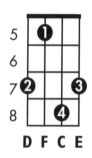

D F C E

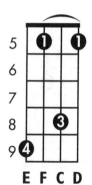

E F C D

D

D7+

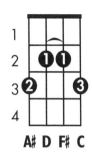

A# D F# C

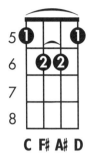

C F# A# D

D7(♭9)

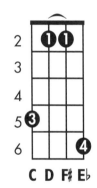

C D F# E♭

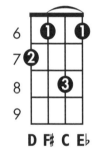

D F# C E♭

D7(#9)

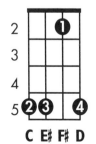

C E# F# D

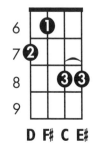

D F# C E#

D

E♭

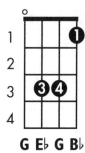

G E♭ G B♭

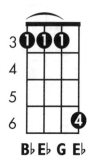

B♭ E♭ G E♭

E♭

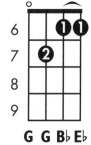

G G B♭ E♭

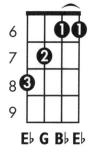

E♭ G B♭ E♭

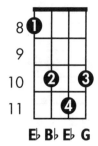

E♭ B♭ E♭ G

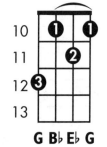

G B♭ E♭ G

E♭m

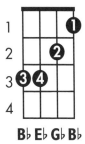

B♭ E♭ G♭ B♭

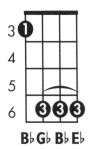

B♭ G♭ B♭ E♭

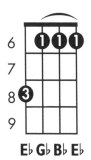

E♭ G♭ B♭ E♭

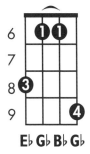

E♭ G♭ B♭ G♭

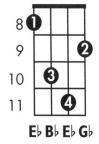

E♭ B♭ E♭ G♭

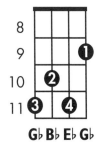

G♭ B♭ E♭ G♭

E♭

135

E♭°

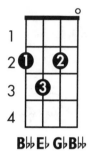

B♭♭ E♭ G♭ B♭♭

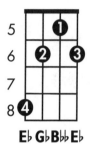

E♭ G♭ B♭♭ E♭

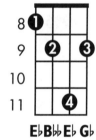

E♭ B♭♭ E♭ G♭

E♭

E♭+

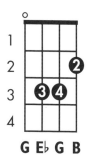

G E♭ G B

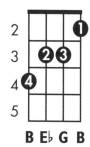

B E♭ G B

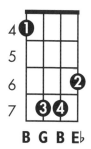

B G B E♭

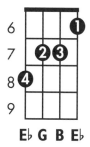

E♭ G B E♭

E♭

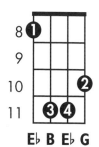

E♭ B E♭ G

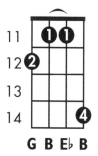

G B E♭ B

E♭5

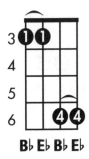

B♭ E♭ B♭ E♭

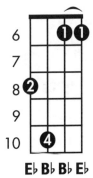

E♭ B♭ B♭ E♭

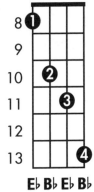

E♭ B♭ E♭ B♭

E♭

138

E♭sus4

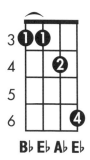

B♭ E♭ A♭ E♭

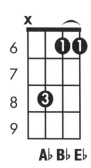

A♭ B♭ E♭

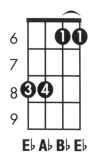

E♭ A♭ B♭ E♭

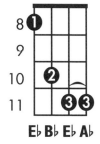

E♭ B♭ E♭ A♭

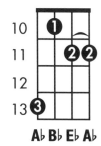

A♭ B♭ E♭ A♭

E♭

E♭6

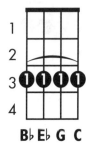

B♭ E♭ G C

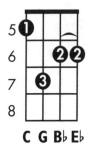

C G B♭ E♭

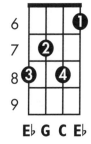

E♭ G C E♭

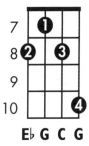

E♭ G C G

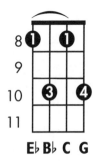

E♭ B♭ C G

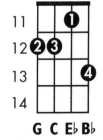

G C E♭ B♭

E♭

E♭m6

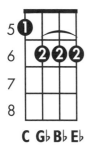

C G♭ B♭ E♭

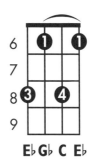

E♭ G♭ C E♭

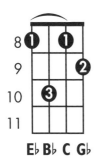

E♭ B♭ C G♭

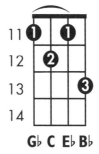

G♭ C E♭ B♭

E♭

E♭7

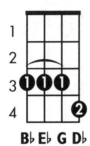

Bb Eb G Db

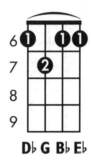

Db G Bb Eb

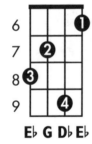

Eb G Db Eb

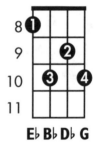

Eb Bb Db G

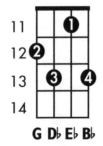

G Db Eb Bb

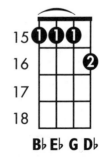

Bb Eb G Db

Eb

E♭maj7

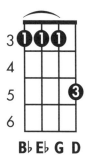

B♭ E♭ G D

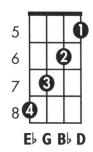

E♭ G B♭ D

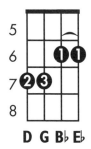

D G B♭ E♭

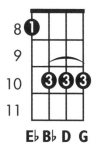

E♭ B♭ D G

E♭

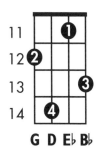

G D E♭ B♭

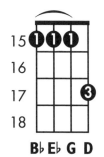

B♭ E♭ G D

143

E♭m7

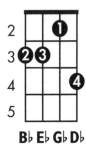

B♭ E♭ G♭ D♭

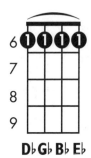

D♭ G♭ B♭ E♭

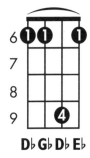

D♭ G♭ D♭ E♭

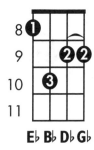

E♭ B♭ D♭ G♭

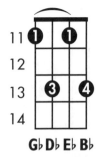

G♭ D♭ E♭ B♭

E♭

144

E♭m7(♭5)

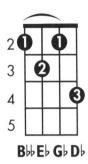

B♭♭ E♭ G♭ D♭

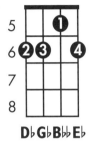

D♭ G♭ B♭♭ E♭

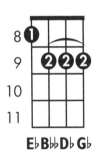

E♭ B♭♭ D♭ G♭

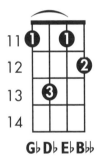

G♭ D♭ E♭ B♭♭

E♭

E♭°7

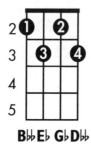

B♭♭ E♭ G♭ D♭♭

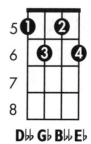

D♭♭ G♭ B♭♭ E♭

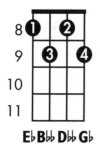

E♭ B♭♭ D♭♭ G♭

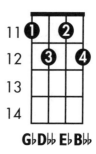

G♭ D♭♭ E♭ B♭♭

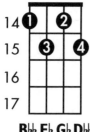

B♭♭ E♭ G♭ D♭♭

E♭

E♭(add9)

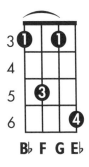

B♭ F G E♭

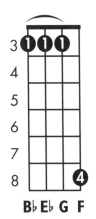

B♭ E♭ G F

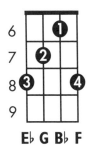

E♭ G B♭ F

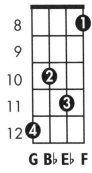

G B♭ E♭ F

E♭

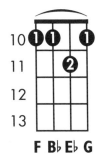

F B♭ E♭ G

147

E♭9

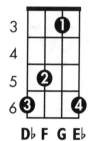

D♭ F G E♭

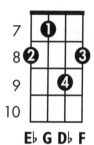

E♭ G D♭ F

E♭maj9

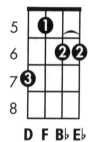

D F B♭ E♭

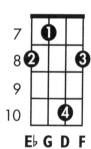

E♭ G D F

E♭m9

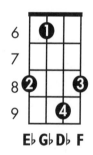

E♭ G♭ D♭ F

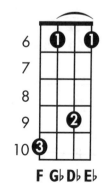

F G♭ D♭ E♭

E♭

E♭7+

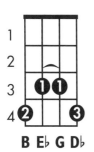

B E♭ G D♭

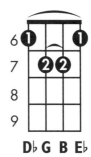

D♭ G B E♭

E♭7(♭9)

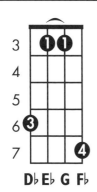

D♭ E♭ G F♭

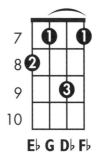

E♭ G D♭ F♭

E♭7(♯9)

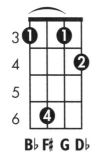

B♭ F♯ G D♭

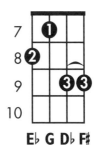

E♭ G D♭ F♯

E♭

E

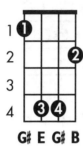

G# E G# B

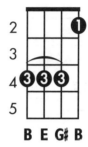

B E G# B

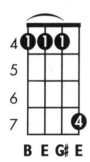

B E G# E

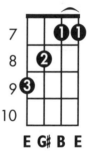

E G# B E

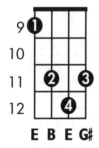

E B E G#

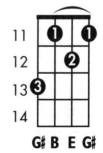

G# B E G#

E

Em

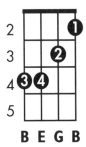

B E G B

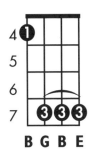

B G B E

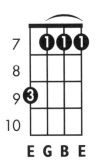

E G B E

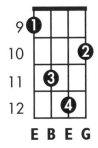

E B E G

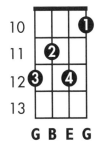

G B E G

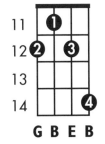

G B E B

E

E°

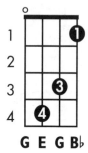

G E G B♭

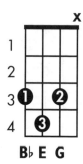

B♭ E G

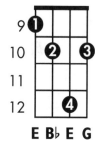

E B♭ E G

E

E+

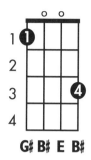

G# B# E B#

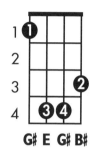

G# E G# B#

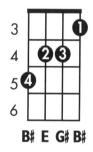

B# E G# B#

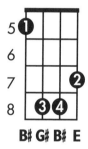

B# G# B# E

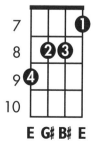

E G# B# E

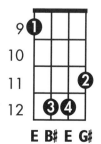

E B# E G#

E5

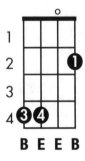

B E E B

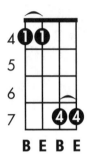

B E B E

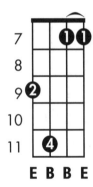

E B B E

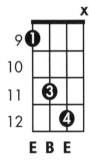

E B E

E

154

Esus4

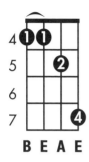

4 B E A E

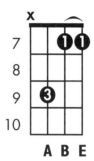

A B E

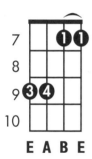

E A B E

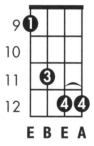

E B E A

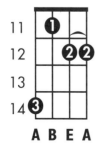

A B E A

E

E6

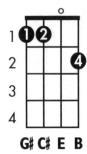

G# C# E B

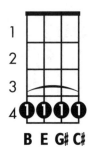

B E G# C#

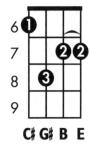

C# G# B E

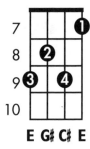

E G# C# E

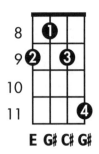

E G# C# G#

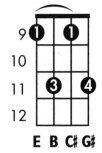

E B C# G#

Em6

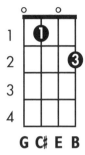

G C♯ E B

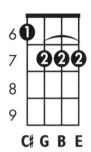

C♯ G B E

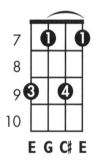

E G C♯ E

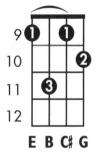

E B C♯ G

E

E7

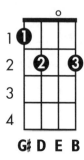

G# D E B

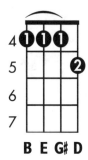

B E G# D

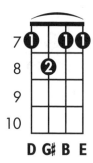

D G# B E

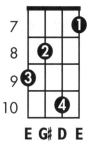

E G# D E

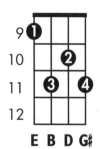

E B D G#

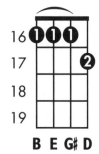

B E G# D

E

Emaj7

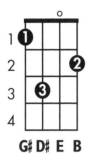

G# D# E B

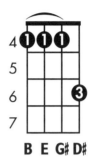

B E G# D#

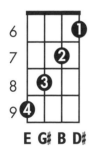

E G# B D#

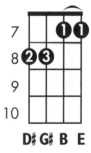

D# G# B E

E

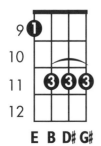

E B D# G#

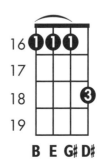

B E G# D#

159

Em7

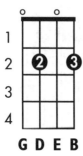

G D E B

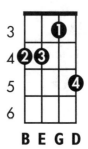

B E G D

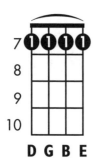

D G B E

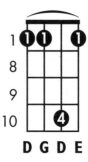

D G D E

E

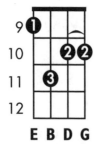

E B D G

160

Em7(♭5)

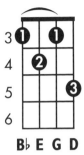

B♭ E G D

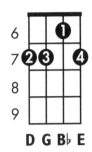

D G B♭ E

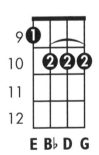

E B♭ D G

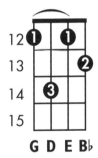

G D E B♭

E

E°7

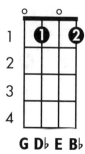

G Db E Bb

B♭ E G Db

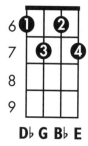

Db G Bb E

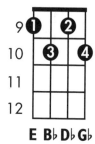

E Bb Db Gb

E

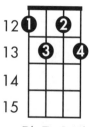

B♭ E G Db

E(add9)

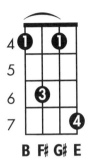

B F# G# E

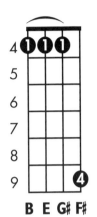

B E G# F#

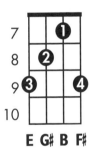

E G# B F#

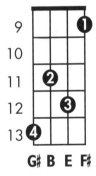

G# B E F#

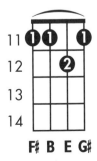

F# B E G#

E

E9

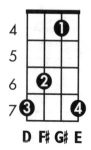

D F# G# E

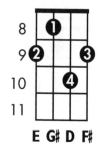

E G# D F#

Emaj9

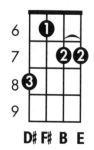

D# F# B E

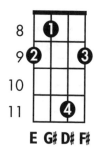

E G# D# F#

E

Em9

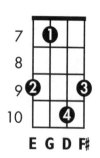

E G D F#

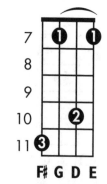

F# G D E

E7+

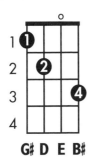

G# D E B#

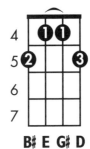

B# E G# D

E7(♭9)

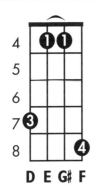

D E G# F

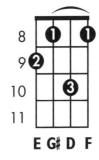

E G# D F

E7(#9)

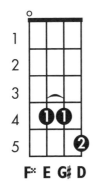

F✳ E G# D

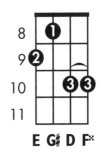

E G# D F✳

E

F

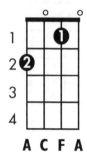

A C F A

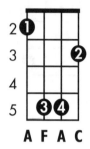

A F A C

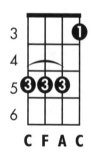

C F A C

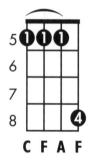

C F A F

F

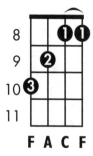

F A C F

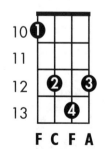

F C F A

166

Fm

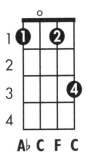

Ab C F C

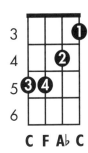

C F Ab C

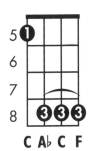

C Ab C F

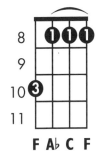

F Ab C F

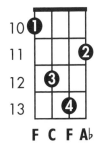

F C F Ab

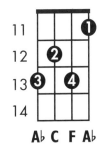

Ab C F Ab

F

F°

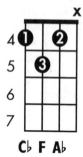

Cb F Ab

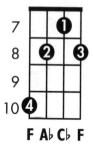

F Ab Cb F

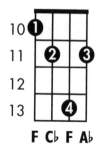

F Cb F Ab

F

F+

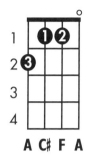

A C# F A

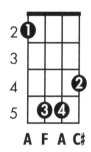

A F A C#

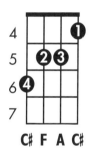

C# F A C#

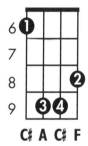

C# A C# F

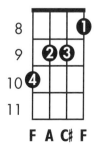

F A C# F

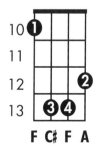

F C# F A

169

F5

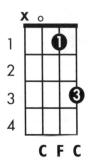

C F C

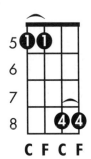

C F C F

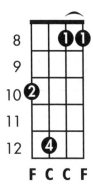

F C C F

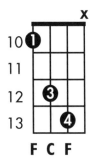

F C F

F

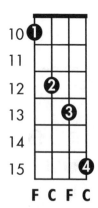

F C F C

170

Fsus4

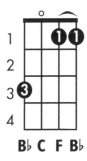

B♭ C F B♭

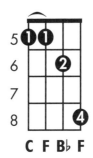

C F B♭ F

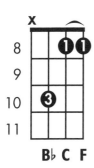

B♭ C F

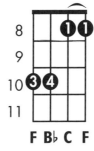

F B♭ C F

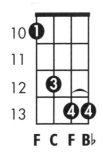

F C F B♭

F6

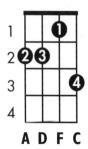

1
2
3
4

A D F C

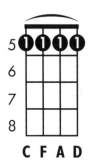

5
6
7
8

C F A D

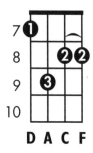

7
8
9
10

D A C F

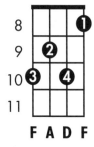

8
9
10
11

F A D F

F

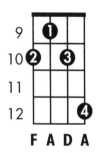

9
10
11
12

F A D A

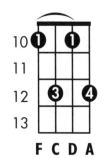

10
11
12
13

F C D A

Fm6

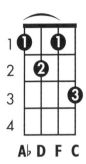

A♭ D F C

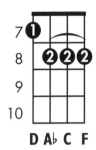

D A♭ C F

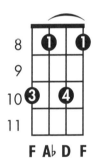

F A♭ D F

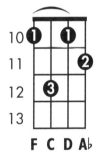

F C D A♭

F

F7

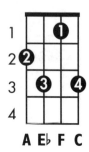

1
2
3
4

A E♭ F C

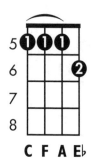

5
6
7
8

C F A E♭

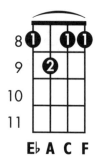

8
9
10
11

E♭ A C F

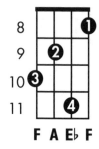

8
9
10
11

F A E♭ F

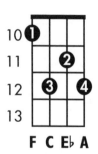

10
11
12
13

F C E♭ A

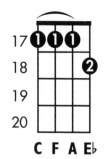

17
18
19
20

C F A E♭

F

174

Fmaj7

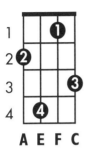

A E F C

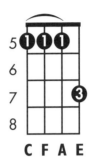

C F A E

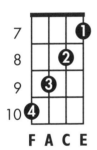

F A C E

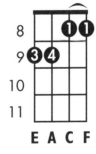

E A C F

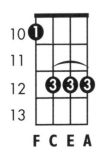

F C E A

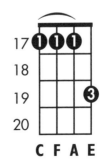

C F A E

F

Fm7

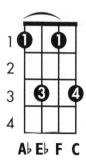

A♭ E♭ F C

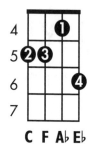

C F A♭ E♭

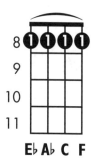

E♭ A♭ C F

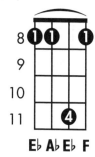

E♭ A♭ E♭ F

F

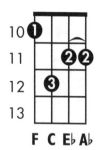

F C E♭ A♭

Fm7(♭5)

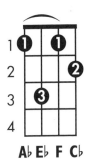

Ab Eb F Cb

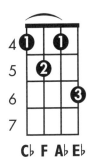

Cb F Ab Eb

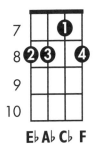

Eb Ab Cb F

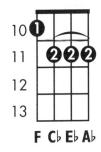

F Cb Eb Ab

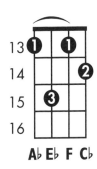

Ab Eb F Cb

F

F°7

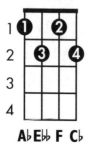

A♭ E♭♭ F C♭

4
5
6
7

C♭ F A♭ E♭♭

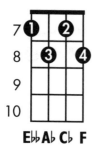

E♭♭ A♭ C♭ F

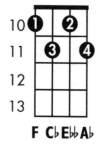

F C♭ E♭♭ A♭

F

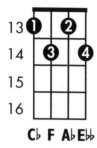

C♭ F A♭ E♭♭

F(add9)

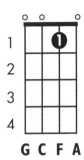

G C F A

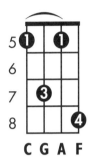

C G A F

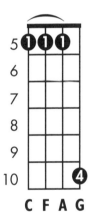

C F A G

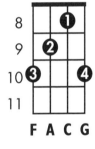

F A C G

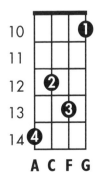

A C F G

F

F9

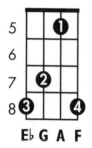

Eb G A F

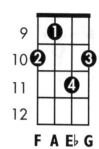

F A Eb G

Fmaj9

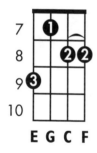

E G C F

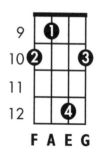

F A E G

Fm9

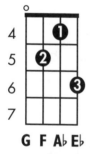

G F Ab Eb

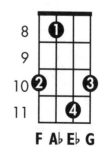

F Ab Eb G

F

F7+

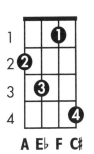

A E♭ F C♯

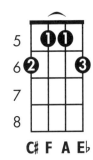

C♯ F A E♭

F7(♭9)

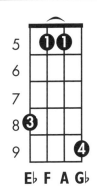

E♭ F A G♭

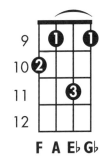

F A E♭ G♭

F7(♯9)

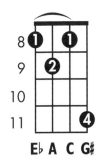

E♭ A C G♯

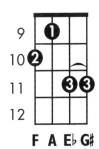

F A E♭ G♯

181

F#

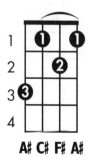

A# C# F# A#

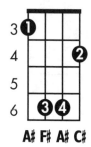

A# F# A# C#

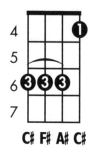

C# F# A# C#

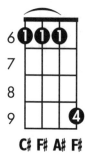

C# F# A# F#

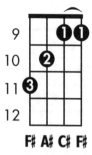

F# A# C# F#

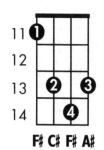

F# C# F# A#

F#m

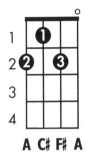

A C# F# A

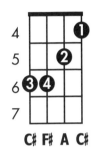

C# F# A C#

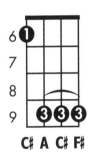

C# A C# F#

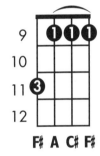

F# A C# F#

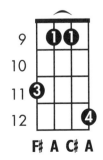

F# A C# A

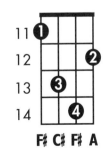

F# C# F# A

F#°

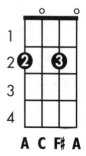

A C F# A

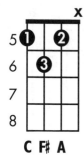

C F# A

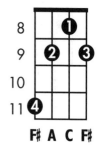

F# A C F#

F#

184

F♯+

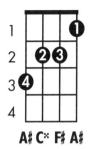

A♯ C✕ F♯ A♯

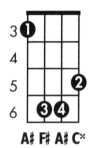

A♯ F♯ A♯ C✕

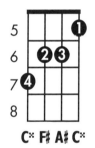

C✕ F♯ A♯ C✕

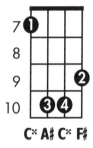

C✕ A♯ C✕ F♯

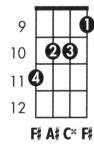

F♯ A♯ C✕ F♯

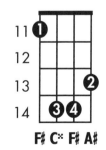

F♯ C✕ F♯ A♯

F♯

185

F#5

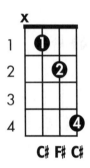

C# F# C#

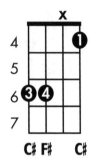

C# F#   C#

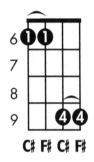

C# F# C# F#

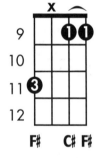

F#   C# F#

F#

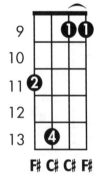

F# C# C# F#

186

F#sus4

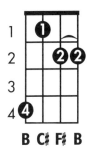

B C# F# B

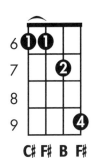

C# F# B F#

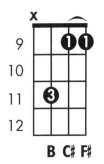

B C# F#

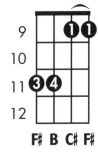

F# B C# F#

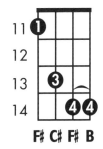

F# C# F# B

F#

F#6

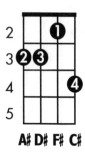

A# D# F# C#

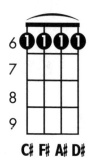

C# F# A# D#

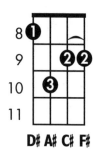

D# A# C# F#

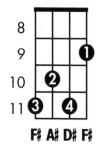

F# A# D# F#

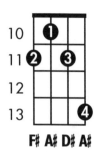

F# A# D# A#

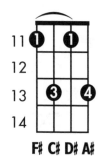

F# C# D# A#

F#m6

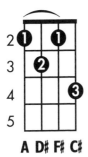

A D# F# C#

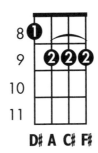

D# A C# F#

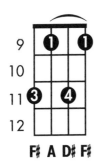

F# A D# F#

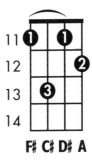

F# C# D# A

F#

F#7

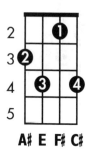

A# E F# C#

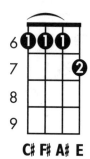

C# F# A# E

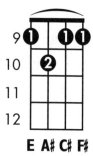

E A# C# F#

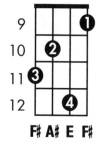

F# A# E F#

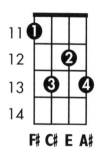

F# C# E A#

F#

F#maj7

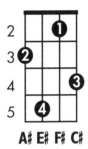

A# E# F# C#

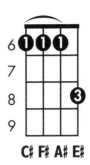

C# F# A# E#

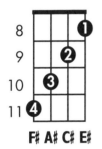

F# A# C# E#

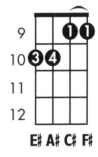

E# A# C# F#

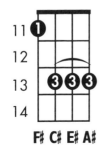

F# C# E# A#

191

F#m7

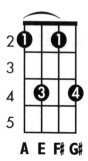

A E F# G#

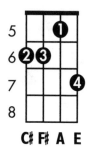

C# F# A E

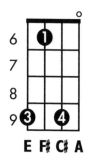

E F# C# A

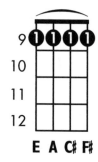

E A C# F#

F#

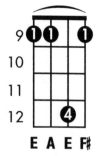

E A E F#

192

F#m7(♭5)

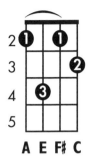

A E F# C

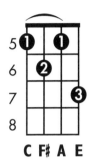

C F# A E

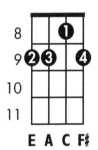

E A C F#

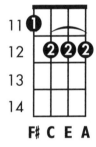

F# C E A

F#

193

F#°7

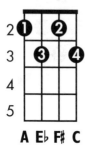

A E♭ F# C

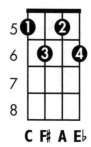

C F# A E♭

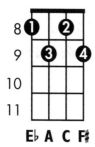

E♭ A C F#

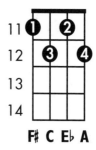

F# C E♭ A

F#

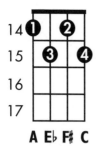

A E♭ F# C

F♯(add9)

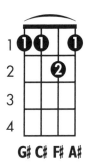

G♯ C♯ F♯ A♯

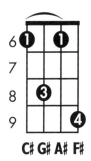

C♯ G♯ A♯ F♯

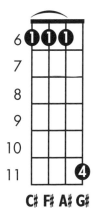

C♯ F♯ A♯ G♯

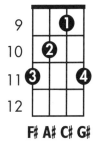

F♯ A♯ C♯ G♯

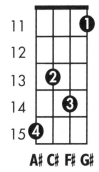

A♯ C♯ F♯ G♯

F♯

F#9

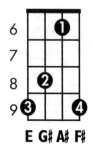

E G# A# F#

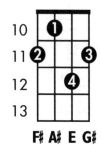

F# A# E G#

F#maj9

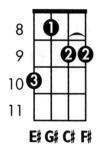

E# G# C# F#

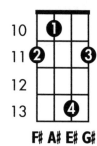

F# A# E# G#

F#m9

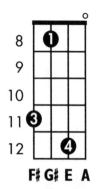

F# G# E A

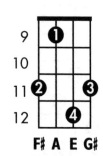

F# A E G#

F#

F#7+

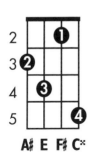

A# E F# C×

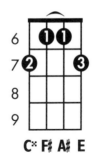

C× F# A# E

F#7(♭9)

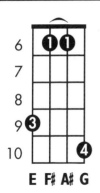

E F# A# G

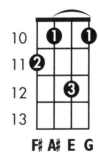

F# A# E G

F#7(#9)

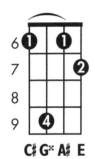

C# G× A# E

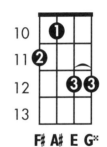

F# A# E G×

F#

G

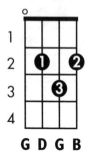

G D G B

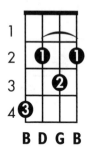

B D G B

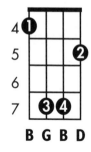

B G B D

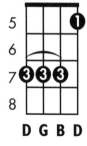

D G B D

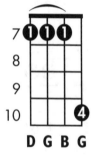

D G B G

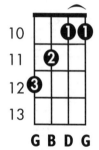

G B D G

G

Gm

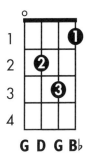

G D G B♭

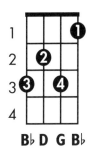

B♭ D G B♭

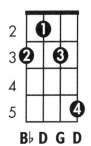

B♭ D G D

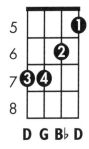

D G B♭ D

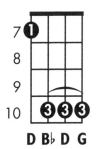

D B♭ D G

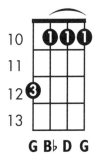

G B♭ D G

G

G°

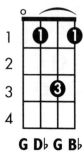

G D♭ G B♭

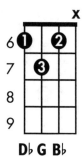

D♭ G B♭

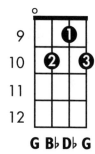

G B♭ D♭ G

G

G+

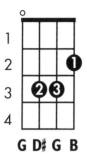

G D# G B

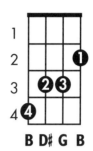

B D# G B

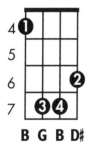

B G B D#

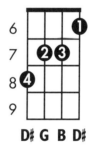

D# G B D#

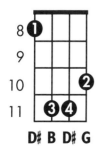

D# B D# G

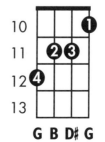

G B D# G

G

201

G5

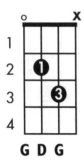

G D G

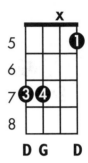

D G D

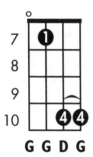

G G D G

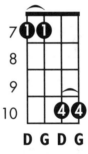

D G D G

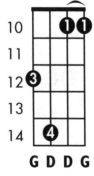

G D D G

G

Gsus4

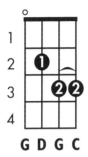

G D G C

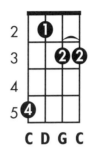

C D G C

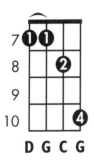

D G C G

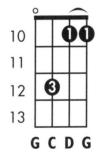

G C D G

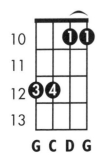

G C D G

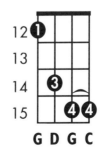

G D G C

G6

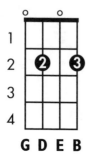

G D E B

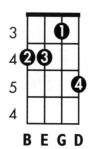

B E G D

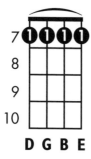

D G B E

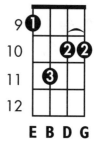

E B D G

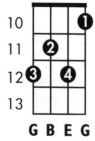

G B E G

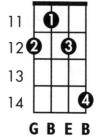

G B E B

G

Gm6

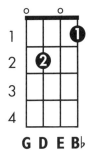

G D E B♭

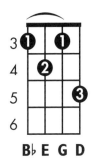

B♭ E G D

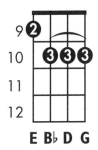

E B♭ D G

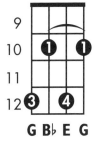

G B♭ E G

G

G7

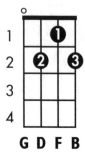

G D F B

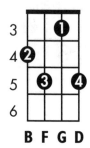

B F G D

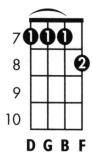

D G B F

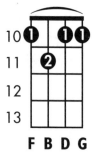

F B D G

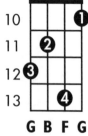

G B F G

G

Gmaj7

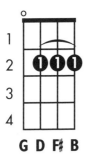

G D F# B

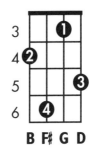

B F# G D

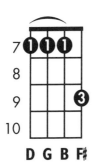

D G B F#

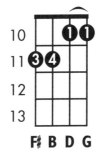

F# B D G

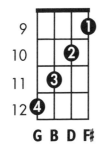

G B D F#

G

Gm7

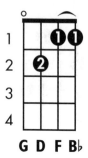

G D F B♭

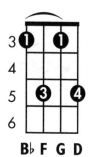

B♭ F G D

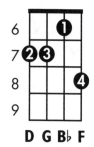

D G B♭ F

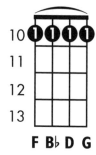

F B♭ D G

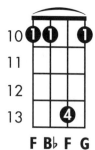

F B♭ F G

G

Gm7(♭5)

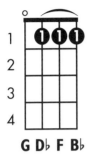

G D♭ F B♭

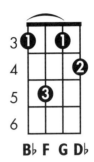

B♭ F G D♭

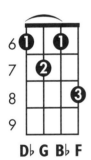

D♭ G B♭ F

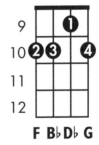

F B♭ D♭ G

G

G°7

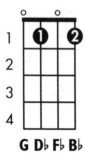

G D♭ F♭ B♭

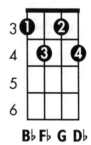

B♭ F♭ G D♭

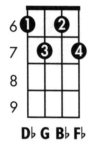

D♭ G B♭ F♭

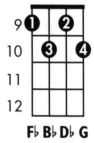

F♭ B♭ D♭ G

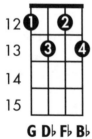

G D♭ F♭ B♭

G

G(add9)

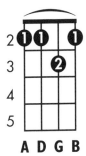

A D G B

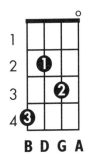

B D G A

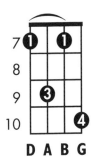

D A B G

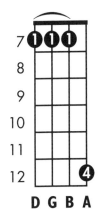

D G B A

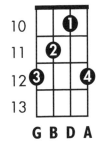

G B D A

G

211

G9

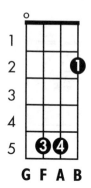

G F A B

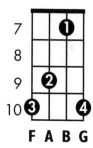

F A B G

Gmaj9

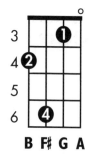

B F♯ G A

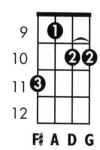

F♯ A D G

Gm9

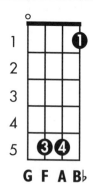

G F A B♭

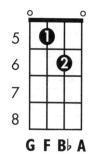

G F B♭ A

G

G7+

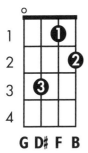

G D♯ F B

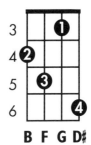

B F G D♯

G7(♭9)

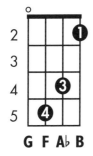

G F A♭ B

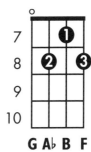

G A♭ B F

G7(♯9)

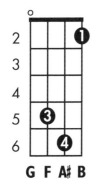

G F A♯ B

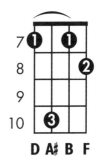

D A♯ B F

G

Moveable Chords

Definitions

These chords are called "moveable" because once a single fingering formation is learned, it can be moved up and down the fingerboard. In this way, a single fingering can be used for as many as 12 different chords.

A *barre* means to hold down two or more strings using only one finger. If the finger holds down all four strings, the barre is called "full."

Roots and Moveable Chords

Every chord has a *root*. The root is the note that names the chord. For example, the root of an E major chord is the note E; the root of an A minor chord is the note A; the root of a C7 chord is the note C, and so on.

When using moveable chords, it is important to remember that, regardless of the fret on which the chord is played, the root always remains on the same string.

In the example below, the root of the B major chord is B. This note is found on the 4th string.

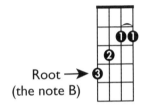

Root → (the note B)

Since the name of the note on the 4th string is B, and since we started with a moveable form of a major chord, the name of this chord is B major. If we move the chord up one more fret, the root is still found on the 4th string. The note is C and the chord is now C major.

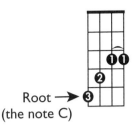

Root → (the note C)

In the following pages, you will learn how to play nine different types of moveable chords, each of which has a fingering with the root on the 4th string, 3rd string, and 2nd string. So, in total, you will learn 27 different fingerings (9x3).

By applying the same method discussed above, you can play 12 different chords with each fingering. Multiply 12 by 27 (the total number of fingerings in this section), and you have 324—the number of chords you will be able to play by learning only 27 fingerings and the notes on the fingerboard.

NOTE: To review the notes on the fingerboard, you can refer to the illustration on page 232.

Moveable Major Chord
(With the Root on the 4th String)

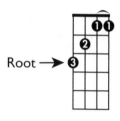

Root →

	With Root At:		
	3rd fret	=	Bb (A#)
	4th fret	=	B
	5th fret	=	C
	6th fret	=	C# (Db)
	7th fret	=	D
	8th fret	=	Eb (D#)
	9th fret	=	E
	10th fret	=	F
	11th fret	=	F# (Gb)
	12th fret	=	G
	13th fret	=	Ab (G#)
	14th fret	=	A

Moveable Major Chord
(With the Root on the 3rd String)

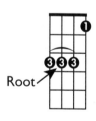

Root

	With Root At:		
	3rd fret	=	Eb (D#)
	4th fret	=	E
	5th fret	=	F
	6th fret	=	F# (Gb)
	7th fret	=	G
	8th fret	=	Ab (G#)
	9th fret	=	A
	10th fret	=	Bb (A#)
	11th fret	=	B
	12th fret	=	C
	13th fret	=	C# (Db)
	14th fret	=	D

Moveable Major Chord
(With the Root on the 2nd String)

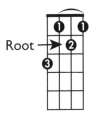

Root →

With Root At:		
2nd fret	=	F# (G♭)
3rd fret	=	G
4th fret	=	A♭ (G#)
5th fret	=	A
6th fret	=	B♭ (A#)
7th fret	=	B
8th fret	=	C
9th fret	=	C# (D♭)
10th fret	=	D
11th fret	=	E♭ (D#)
12th fret	=	E
13th fret	=	F

Moveable Minor Chord
(With the Root on the 4th String)

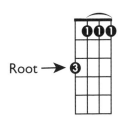

Root →

With Root At:		
3rd fret	=	B♭m (A#m)
4th fret	=	Bm
5th fret	=	Cm
6th fret	=	C#m (D♭m)
7th fret	=	Dm
8th fret	=	E♭m (D#m)
9th fret	=	Em
10th fret	=	Fm
11th fret	=	F#m (G♭m)
12th fret	=	Gm
13th fret	=	A♭m (G#m)
14th fret	=	Am

Moveable Minor Chord
(With the Root on the 3rd String)

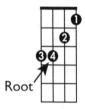

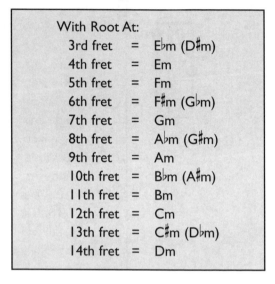

With Root At:

3rd fret	=	E♭m (D♯m)
4th fret	=	Em
5th fret	=	Fm
6th fret	=	F♯m (G♭m)
7th fret	=	Gm
8th fret	=	A♭m (G♯m)
9th fret	=	Am
10th fret	=	B♭m (A♯m)
11th fret	=	Bm
12th fret	=	Cm
13th fret	=	C♯m (D♭m)
14th fret	=	Dm

Moveable Minor Chord
(With the Root on the 2nd String)

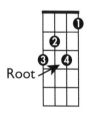

With Root At:

3rd fret	=	Gm
4th fret	=	A♭m (G♯m)
5th fret	=	Am
6th fret	=	B♭m (A♯m)
7th fret	=	Bm
8th fret	=	Cm
9th fret	=	C♯m (D♭m)
10th fret	=	Dm
11th fret	=	E♭m (D♯m)
12th fret	=	Em
13th fret	=	Fm
14th fret	=	F♯m (G♭m)

Moveable 5th Chord
(With the Root on the 4th String)

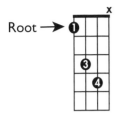

Root →

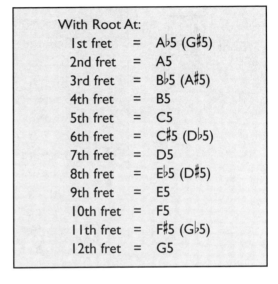

With Root At:

1st fret	=	A♭5 (G♯5)
2nd fret	=	A5
3rd fret	=	B♭5 (A♯5)
4th fret	=	B5
5th fret	=	C5
6th fret	=	C♯5 (D♭5)
7th fret	=	D5
8th fret	=	E♭5 (D♯5)
9th fret	=	E5
10th fret	=	F5
11th fret	=	F♯5 (G♭5)
12th fret	=	G5

Moveable 5th Chord
(With the Root on the 3rd String)

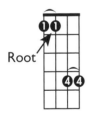

Root

With Root At:

1st fret	=	C♯5 (D♭5)
2nd fret	=	D5
3rd fret	=	E♭5 (D♯5)
4th fret	=	E5
5th fret	=	F5
6th fret	=	F♯5 (G♭5)
7th fret	=	G5
8th fret	=	A♭5 (G♯5)
9th fret	=	A5
10th fret	=	B♭5 (A♯5)
11th fret	=	B5
12th fret	=	C5

Moveable 5th Chord
(With the Root on the 2nd String)

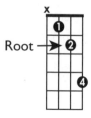

Root →

With Root At:		
2nd fret	=	F#5 (G♭5)
3rd fret	=	G5
4th fret	=	A♭5 (G#5)
5th fret	=	A5
6th fret	=	B♭5 (A#5)
7th fret	=	B5
8th fret	=	C5
9th fret	=	C#5 (D♭5)
10th fret	=	D5
11th fret	=	E♭5 (D#5)
12th fret	=	E5
13th fret	=	F5

Moveable 6th Chord
(With the Root on the 4th String)

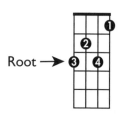

Root →

With Root At:		
3rd fret	=	B♭6 (A#6)
4th fret	=	B6
5th fret	=	C6
6th fret	=	C#6 (D♭6)
7th fret	=	D6
8th fret	=	E♭6 (D#6)
9th fret	=	E6
10th fret	=	F6
11th fret	=	F#6 (G♭6)
12th fret	=	G6
13th fret	=	A♭6 (G#6)
14th fret	=	A6

Moveable 6th Chord
(With the Root on the 3rd String)

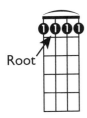

Root

With Root At:		
1st fret	=	C#6 (Db6)
2nd fret	=	D6
3rd fret	=	Eb6 (D#6)
4th fret	=	E6
5th fret	=	F6
6th fret	=	F#6 (Gb6)
7th fret	=	G6
8th fret	=	Ab6 (G#6)
9th fret	=	A6
10th fret	=	Bb6 (A#6)
11th fret	=	B6
12th fret	=	C6

Moveable 6th Chord
(With the Root on the 2nd String)

Root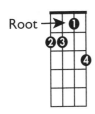

With Root At:		
1st fret	=	F6
2nd fret	=	F#6 (Gb6)
3rd fret	=	G6
4th fret	=	Ab6 (G#6)
5th fret	=	A6
6th fret	=	Bb6 (A#6)
7th fret	=	B6
8th fret	=	C6
9th fret	=	C#6 (Db6)
10th fret	=	D6
11th fret	=	Eb6 (D#6)
12th fret	=	E6

Moveable Minor 6th Chord
(With the Root on the 4th String)

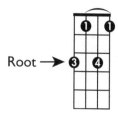

Root →

With Root At:

3rd fret	=	B♭m6 (A♯m6)
4th fret	=	Bm6
5th fret	=	Cm6
6th fret	=	C♯m6 (D♭m6)
7th fret	=	Dm6
8th fret	=	E♭m6 (D♯m6)
9th fret	=	Em6
10th fret	=	Fm6
11th fret	=	F♯m6 (G♭m6)
12th fret	=	Gm6
13th fret	=	A♭m6 (G♯m6)
14th fret	=	Am6

Moveable Minor 6th Chord
(With the Root on the 3rd String)

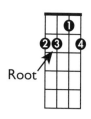

Root

With Root At:

2nd fret	=	Dm6
3rd fret	=	E♭m6 (D♯m6)
4th fret	=	Em6
5th fret	=	Fm6
6th fret	=	F♯m6 (G♭m6)
7th fret	=	Gm6
8th fret	=	A♭m6 (G♯m6)
9th fret	=	Am6
10th fret	=	B♭m6 (A♯m6)
11th fret	=	Bm6
12th fret	=	Cm6
13th fret	=	C♯m6 (D♭m6)

Moveable Minor 6th Chord
(With the Root on the 2nd String)

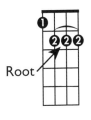

Root

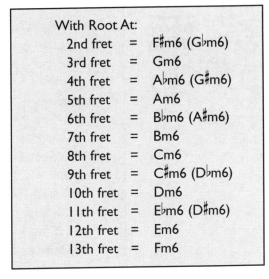

With Root At:		
2nd fret	=	F#m6 (G♭m6)
3rd fret	=	Gm6
4th fret	=	A♭m6 (G#m6)
5th fret	=	Am6
6th fret	=	B♭m6 (A#m6)
7th fret	=	Bm6
8th fret	=	Cm6
9th fret	=	C#m6 (D♭m6)
10th fret	=	Dm6
11th fret	=	E♭m6 (D#m6)
12th fret	=	Em6
13th fret	=	Fm6

Moveable 7th Chord
(With Root on the 4th String)

Root →

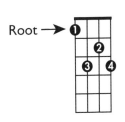

With Root At:		
1st fret	=	A♭7 (G#7)
2nd fret	=	A7
3rd fret	=	B♭7 (A#7)
4th fret	=	B7
5th fret	=	C7
6th fret	=	C#7 (D♭7)
7th fret	=	D7
8th fret	=	E♭7 (D#7)
9th fret	=	E7
10th fret	=	F7
11th fret	=	F#7 (G♭7)
12th fret	=	G7

Moveable 7th Chord
(With Root on the 3rd String)

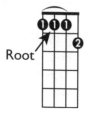

Root

With Root At:		
1st fret	=	C#7 (D♭7)
2nd fret	=	D7
3rd fret	=	E♭7 (D#7)
4th fret	=	E7
5th fret	=	F7
6th fret	=	F#7 (G♭7)
7th fret	=	G7
8th fret	=	A♭7 (G#7)
9th fret	=	A7
10th fret	=	B♭7 (A#7)
11th fret	=	B7
12th fret	=	C7

Moveable 7th Chord
(With Root on the 2nd String)

Root →

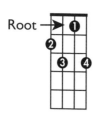

With Root At:		
1st fret	=	F7
2nd fret	=	F#7 (G♭7)
3rd fret	=	G7
4th fret	=	A♭7 (G#7)
5th fret	=	A7
6th fret	=	B♭7 (A#7)
7th fret	=	B7
8th fret	=	C7
9th fret	=	C#7 (D♭7)
10th fret	=	D7
11th fret	=	E♭7 (D#7)
12th fret	=	E7

Moveable Major 7th Chord
(With the Root on the 4th String)

Root →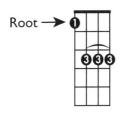

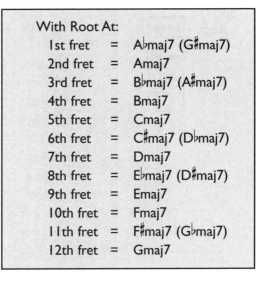

With Root At:

1st fret	=	A♭maj7 (G♯maj7)
2nd fret	=	Amaj7
3rd fret	=	B♭maj7 (A♯maj7)
4th fret	=	Bmaj7
5th fret	=	Cmaj7
6th fret	=	C♯maj7 (D♭maj7)
7th fret	=	Dmaj7
8th fret	=	E♭maj7 (D♯maj7)
9th fret	=	Emaj7
10th fret	=	Fmaj7
11th fret	=	F♯maj7 (G♭maj7)
12th fret	=	Gmaj7

Moveable Major 7th Chord
(With the Root on the 3rd String)

Root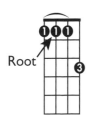

With Root At:

1st fret	=	C♯maj7 (D♭maj7)
2nd fret	=	Dmaj7
3rd fret	=	E♭maj7 (D♯maj7)
4th fret	=	Emaj7
5th fret	=	Fmaj7
6th fret	=	F♯maj7 (G♭maj7)
7th fret	=	Gmaj7
8th fret	=	A♭maj7 (G♯maj7)
9th fret	=	Amaj7
10th fret	=	B♭maj7 (A♯maj7)
11th fret	=	Bmaj7
12th fret	=	Cmaj7

Moveable Major 7th Chord
(With the Root on the 2nd String)

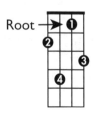

With Root At:		
1st fret	=	Fmaj7
2nd fret	=	F#maj7 (G♭maj7)
3rd fret	=	Gmaj7
4th fret	=	A♭maj7 (G#maj7)
5th fret	=	Amaj7
6th fret	=	B♭maj7 (A#maj7)
7th fret	=	Bmaj7
8th fret	=	Cmaj7
9th fret	=	C#maj7 (D♭maj7)
10th fret	=	Dmaj7
11th fret	=	E♭maj7 (D#maj7)
12th fret	=	Emaj7

Moveable Minor 7th Chord
(With the Root on the 4th String)

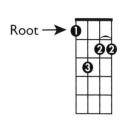

With Root At:		
1st fret	=	A♭m7 (G#m7)
2nd fret	=	Am7
3rd fret	=	B♭m7 (A#m7)
4th fret	=	Bm7
5th fret	=	Cm7
6th fret	=	C#m7 (D♭m7)
7th fret	=	Dm7
8th fret	=	E♭m7 (D#m7)
9th fret	=	Em7
10th fret	=	Fm7
11th fret	=	F#m7 (G♭m7)
12th fret	=	Gm7

Moveable Minor 7th Chord
(With the Root on the 3rd String)

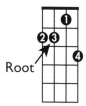

Root

With Root At:

2nd fret	=	Dm7
3rd fret	=	E♭m7 (D♯m7)
4th fret	=	Em7
5th fret	=	Fm7
6th fret	=	F♯m7 (G♭m7)
7th fret	=	Gm7
8th fret	=	A♭m7 (G♯m7)
9th fret	=	Am7
10th fret	=	B♭m7 (A♯m7)
11th fret	=	Bm7
12th fret	=	Cm7
13th fret	=	C♯m7 (D♭m7)

Moveable Minor 7th Chord
(With the Root on the 2nd String)

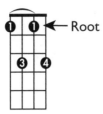

← Root

With Root At:

1st fret	=	Fm7
2nd fret	=	F#m7 (G♭m7)
3rd fret	=	Gm7
4th fret	=	A♭m7 (G#m7)
5th fret	=	Am7
6th fret	=	B♭m7 (A#m7)
7th fret	=	Bm7
8th fret	=	Cm7
9th fret	=	C#m7 (D♭m7)
10th fret	=	Dm7
11th fret	=	E♭m7 (D#m7)
12th fret	=	Em7

Moveable 9th Chord
(With the Root on the 4th String)

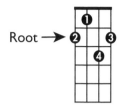

Root →

With Root At:

2nd fret	=	A9
3rd fret	=	B♭9 (A♯9)
4th fret	=	B9
5th fret	=	C9
6th fret	=	C♯9 (D♭9)
7th fret	=	D9
8th fret	=	E♭9 (D♯9)
9th fret	=	E9
10th fret	=	F9
11th fret	=	F♯9 (G♭9)
12th fret	=	G9
13th fret	=	A♭9 (G♯9)

Moveable 9th Chord
(With the Root on the 3rd String)

Root →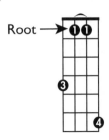

With Root At:		
1st fret	=	C♯9 (D♭9)
2nd fret	=	D9
3rd fret	=	E♭9 (D♯9)
4th fret	=	E9
5th fret	=	F9
6th fret	=	F♯9 (G♭9)
7th fret	=	G9
8th fret	=	A♭9 (G♯9)
9th fret	=	A9
10th fret	=	B♭9 (A♯9)
11th fret	=	B9
12th fret	=	C9

Moveable 9th Chord
(With the Root on the 2nd String)

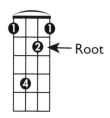 ← Root

With Root At:
2nd fret	=	F#9 (G♭9)
3rd fret	=	G9
4th fret	=	A♭9 (G#9)
5th fret	=	A9
6th fret	=	B♭9 (A#9)
7th fret	=	B9
8th fret	=	C9
9th fret	=	C#9 (D♭9)
10th fret	=	D9
11th fret	=	E♭9 (D#9)
12th fret	=	E9
13th fret	=	F9

Ukulele Fingerboard Chart
Frets 1–12

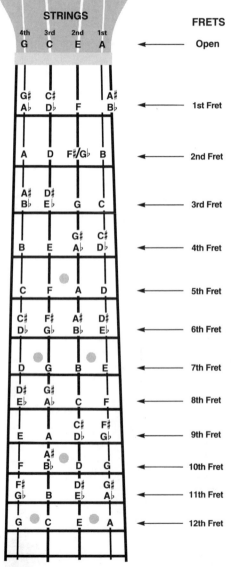

STRINGS

4th	3rd	2nd	1st
G	C	E	A

FRETS

← Open

G♯/A♭ C♯/D♭ F A♯/B♭ ← 1st Fret

A D F♯/G♭ B ← 2nd Fret

A♯/B♭ D♯/E♭ G C ← 3rd Fret

G♯/A♭ C♯/D♭
B E ← 4th Fret

C F A D ← 5th Fret

C♯/D♭ F♯/G♭ A♯/B♭ D♯/E♭ ← 6th Fret

D G B E ← 7th Fret

D♯/E♭ G♯/A♭ C F ← 8th Fret

C♯/D♭ F♯/G♭
E A ← 9th Fret

A♯/B♭
F D G ← 10th Fret

F♯/G♭ B D♯/E♭ G♯/A♭ ← 11th Fret

G C E A ← 12th Fret